EAT
THE GRAPES
DOWNWARD

EAT
THE GRAPES
DOWNWARD

*An Uninhibited Romp
Through the Surprising World of Food*

Vernon Pizer

DODD, MEAD & COMPANY · NEW YORK

1   2   3   4   5   6   7   8   9   10

Library of Congress Cataloging in Publication Data

Pizer, Vernon, date
Eat the grapes downward.

Includes index.
Summary: Presents fact, fiction, myths, and
anecdotes from many places and time periods—all
concerning food.
1. Food.   2. Gastronomy.   [1. Food.   2. Gastronomy]
I. Title.
TX353.P48   1983   641′.01′3   83-11569
ISBN 0-396-08203-3

*Always eat grapes
downward—that is, always eat
the best grapes first;
in this way there will be none
better left on the bunch,
and each grape will seem good
down to the last.
If you eat the other way,
you will not have
a good grape in the lot.*

SAMUEL BUTLER

Other Books by Vernon Pizer

TAKE MY WORD FOR IT

GLORIOUS TRIUMPHS:
Athletes Who Conquered Adversity

SHORTCHANGED BY HISTORY:
America's Neglected Innovators

YOU DON'T SAY:
How People Communicate Without Speech

INK, ARK., AND ALL THAT:
How American Places Got Their Names

THE UNITED STATES ARMY

THE WORLD OCEAN:
Man's Last Frontier

THE USEFUL ATOM
(with William R. Anderson)

ROCKETS, MISSILES AND SPACE

IT WOULD BE UNFAIR and ill-mannered of me to neglect acknowledging and publicly thanking all who contributed factual background and anecdotal material to aid in writing this book. But they are so many that to cite each by name would be to compile a list of unwieldy length. So let me simply issue a blanket expression of gratitude to all who aided so graciously.

Even so there are a few who must be singled out by name: the late Arnold Gingrich, founding editor and guiding genius of *Esquire,* for having encouraged and published some of my earliest articles, and for the memorable meals we shared on two continents; Kay Weisberg, innovative director of the Smithsonian Institution's Insect Zoo, for convincing me that one man's food is another man's poison, and vice versa; and my wife, Marguerite, for her patience and forbearance, drawing the line only at sharing *percebes* in Madrid and lamb's fries in New Orleans.

Vernon Pizer

VALDOSTA · GEORGIA

CONTENTS

Chapter One

THE FIRST BITE

For my part, I mind
my belly most studiously and very
carefully; for I look upon it
that he who does not mind his belly
will hardly mind anything else.

SAMUEL JOHNSON

11

he nineteenth-century French diplomat, Talleyrand, may have been opportunistic and cynical, with morals as elastic as his loyalties, but one cannot deny that he was also a man of wit and perception. When he was speaking once about all of the ways in which mankind seeks its pleasures he insisted that eating should head the list, challenging his listeners to "inform me of any other pleasure which can be enjoyed three times daily, and equally in old age as in youth." Nobody ever accepted his challenge.

Food is what this book is all about. Not how to raise it or gather it, nor how to cook it or process it or distribute it. But food in its own right and for its own sake. Food with its myths and its superstitions, its surprises and contradictions, its wonderful capacity to shed fresh light in a fresh way on people and events, even its humor and its moments of high drama. Food that created empires—and lost them. Food as a social preoccupation, a sexual instrument, a religious sacrament, and the only thing humans fashion into artistic creations intended solely for destruction by their admirers. Food that separates man from other animals because he alone cooks it and will eat even when he does not experience hunger.

If one lives out the proverbial threescore and ten years, each day eating the normal three meals, a staggering 76,650 meals will have been done away with by the time the last earthly morsel is consumed. Logic suggests that anything claiming that much time and attention should have become repetitively routine and commonplace, completely predictable and incapable of springing any surprises. But one of the enduring fascinations of food is that it is illogical and unpredictable. Take, as an example, the world's best known apple, the one that Adam and Eve ate in the Garden of Eden. It now appears that it may not have been an apple at all. The Bible identifies it only as the fruit of the tree of knowledge of good and evil; many modern scholars think it quite likely that what Adam and Eve actually munched on was a pomegranate, while among many Moslems it is identified as a banana.

If it was food that caused Adam and Eve's downfall in Eden, it was also food that made an international criminal of the third President of the United States. In 1784, seven years before he entered the White House, Thomas Jefferson served as American Minister to France where his most urgent task was to establish an export market for American goods. He could arouse French interest in only one product, rice from the plantations of Carolina and Georgia. The trouble was that during the Revolution the British occupying Charleston and Savannah had shipped all of America's rice, including seed stocks, to England. Now, with no seed available, the nation could not produce for the French market. While wrestling with his dilemma, Jefferson learned of the existence of a new and improved Italian strain of rice; he also learned that to prevent its cultivation

by competing nations Italy prohibited its export, imposing harsh penalties for violators. Undaunted, he went to
Italy, obtained two sacks of the grain, and smuggled out
his contraband successfully. Jefferson's illicit rice was the
feedstock that revitalized America's languishing plantations.

Food smuggling seems to have been a fairly general
practice in Jefferson's day. A colleague of his—Colonel
David Humphrey, first American Minister to Spain—
violated Spanish law by spiriting a hundred of that country's superior Merino sheep across the border to Portugal
where he had them loaded aboard a U.S.-bound vessel.

But coffee holds the record for being smuggled and
schemed over. A rigidly controlled crop in Arabia where it
was grown, coffee was closely guarded to prevent access by
foreigners. The first breach came when a traveler from
India risked death to smuggle seed from Arabia to Ceylon
where it was planted and flourished. Then the Dutch
succeeded in making off with seed from Ceylon to Indonesia where again the plantings grew lushly. As the
seventeenth century was winding down, coffee drinking
was popular everywhere but coffee growing was still
tightly controlled. Louis XIV, King of France, didn't like
the idea of having someone able to come between him and
his coffee cup, so he pressured the Dutch into letting him
have a single plant from Indonesia. Louis built a
greenhouse—reputedly Europe's first greenhouse—for the
precious plant and assigned a staff of agricultural nurse-

maids to grow it and to cultivate other plants from its seed. Now Louis was master of his coffee cup.

In 1723 a French naval officer being assigned to duty in Martinique, an island possession in the Caribbean, persuaded the greenhouse superintendent to let him take a plant to his new post. The climate was hospitable to the cultivation of coffee and within a dozen years all of France's Latin-American possessions had thriving plantations. Now Brazil entered the scene. Anxious to start a coffee industry of its own, Brazil sent an agent to French Guiana to buy seed if he could or steal it if he had to. An effective French security system blocked him from doing either, so the agent probed for a weak spot and found it: the governor's wife. He carried on a clandestine romance with the wife and from her obtained the seed that Brazil coveted.

In the realm of food all things are possible. For Jefferson and others food led to crime. However, in ancient China a way was found to use food as a protection against crime. The Chinese had noted that when an individual lies under stress his mouth becomes dry. When questioning a suspect involved in a crime, the authorities exploited this stress-induced dryness by forcing the suspect to chew rice powder to see if he could salivate enough to make it wet. It is only speculation that during one of these interrogation sessions some ancient Chinese policeman coined the command: "Spit it out!"

Food not only illuminates colorful fragments of many of humanity's adventures and misadventures, it is also the prime motivation that stimulated some of them. It has been said—in jest, true enough, but with a little kernel of truth at the core of the jest—that the only reason Caesar invaded Britain in 55 B.C. was to assure himself of uninterrupted access to its succulent oysters. He was, of course, attracted by more of its assets than just the tasty shellfish, but it is fact that he had regularly dispatched agents all the way to Britain to obtain oysters for his table.

There is no question that it was foodstuffs—spices—that launched one of the grandest, most sweeping series of dramas in recorded history. Many spices influenced the ebb and flow of events but the central role was undoubtedly played by pepper, the small berry of an Indian vine that for over 3,000 years has been the world's most important spice. So valued was it that when the Visigoths laid siege to Rome in 408 they demanded tribute paid in peppercorns. Some years after that the English initiated a custom of sewing up the pockets of dockworkers to discourage them from trying to pilfer peppercorns from incoming cargo. So in the fifteenth century when the Turks blocked the overland route to India and its prized pepper crop, an aroused Europe began launching expeditions seeking a sea route bypassing the Turkish blocking force. Thus pepper, most valued of the edible spices, precipitated the great age of discovery that revealed a whole New World and profoundly altered the course of history.

If food gained Europe a New World it was also food that lost one of Europe's rulers his head. Louis XVI had an enormously greedy appetite that nothing could divert, not even the revolution that was breaking out in many parts of France. In 1791, with armed mobs battling their way toward his palace, Louis decided the time had come to seek refuge in the north. But he delayed his departure until he could assure himself that his kitchen staff and a huge store of food and wine were included in his escape caravan. It was midmorning when the group finally departed and by noon Louis could no longer restrain his appetite. Ignoring his advisors, he called a halt for lunch. Even then all might not have been lost had Louis not been so greedy; he insisted on dallying for three hours of nonstop eating, which gave his pursuers time to catch up and return him to Paris where he and his head eventually parted company on the guillotine. (Louis's queen, Marie Antoinette, is also remembered for a food incident. Responding to her starving subjects clamoring for bread, she is supposed to have said cynically, "Let them eat cake." Marie was guilty of many heartless things but uttering that famous remark does not appear to be one of them.)

Since the beginning of recorded history the authorities everywhere seem to have spent much of their time involved with food matters in one way or another. Officials in early Greece attempted to insure conservatism at the dinner table by issuing edicts restricting the size of meals citizens were permitted to eat. The regulations, virtually impossible to enforce effectively, did not seem to have a noticeable effect on consumption. The Romans, learning nothing from the earlier Greek experience with sumptuary laws, passed ordinances limiting the amount inhabitants could spend on meals and prohibiting them from serving more than one unfattened hen when entertaining guests. A fourteenth-century English sumptuary law restricted the number of courses that could be served at dinner. When Henry VIII came along in the fifteenth century he made two demands at his royal table: enormous quantities of food, and dishes flavored with saffron, a scarce spice. To eliminate much of the competitive demand for his favorite spice he issued an edict banning the practice of using saffron to dye beards and hair orange.

Even in the modern world edicts to control food consumption continue to be adopted—and continue to be ignored. Chung Hee Park, the late president of South Korea and evidently no student of the futility of sumptuary laws, decreed that his countrymen must limit dinner to no more than ten courses. This would seem to outsiders to work no hardship but Koreans are noted for routinely dining on as many as twenty courses, admittedly consuming only modest amounts of each dish. They declined to alter their ways, continuing to eat as many courses as they wished and could afford.

Political figures and food have from the beginning had as strong an affinity for one another in America as elsewhere. This affinity was in evidence in the very first holiday created by the Colonial authorities in America: a celebration of food, Thanksgiving. It was a token of things to come. It is not without significance that the first distinctly American word coined in the New World was aimed at the stomach: "chowder."

In the early days of the Republic that masterful orator, Daniel Webster, rose from his seat in the Senate one day to address his colleagues on a matter that was dear to him. Lovingly and lengthily, he declaimed on the virtues of fish chowder. Had Daniel Webster survived to the end of the nineteenth century he would have been heartened by the performance of George Frisbie Hoare, a fellow fish-lover who succeeded him as a member of the Senate. Interrupting debate on proposed pure food legislation, Senator Hoare embarked on long, fulsome praise of "the exquisite flavor of the codfish, salted, made into balls, and eaten on a Sunday morning."

In 1935, during all-night deliberation on a controversial bill, Senator Huey Long took the floor to deliver a minutely detailed description of the proper methods of preparing potlikker, fried oysters, and Roquefort cheese salad dressing. More recently, Senators Goldwater and Tower debated the issue of Arizona versus Texas chili. Going for the jugular, Goldwater charged that "a Texan does not know chili from leavings in the corral." Stung by this attack on the culinary honor of his native state, Tower riposted, "Comparing Arizona chili to Texas chili is like comparing Phyllis Diller with Sophia Loren."

When it comes to a question of food, normalcy often becomes a relative matter—as Congress' culinary antics demonstrate. There are many who would come away from an encounter with the Japanese and their beef similarly convinced that normalcy—like beauty—is sometimes in the eye of the beholder. In 1856, when Townsend Harris arrived in Japan to take up his post as the first U.S. diplomat assigned to that country, he was distressed to discover that nowhere in Japan could he buy beef for his table. It was not that Japan had no cows—it did—but they were used solely as work animals; a Japanese would no more think of eating his cow than an American farmer would think of eating his mule. Finally, a beef-starved Harris succeeded in having a cow butchered for him. After that first chip in the wall of resistance to the cow as food, other cracks began slowly to appear. Ultimately the whole wall came tumbling down and what had once been viewed by the Japanese as the abnormal foreign practice of eating beef became normal throughout the country.

Today there are many connoisseurs who believe that the world's tastiest beef comes from cattle raised in Kobe, Japan. If not the tastiest then certainly these are the most pampered cows to be found anywhere. The Kobe farmers fatten their animals on bottled beer and give them daily massages by hand to distribute the fat through their bodies and to tenderize their flesh. Hawaiians would not find it especially strange that Kobe cows have a daily massage. The Hawaiian delicacy, lomi lomi, is prepared from salmon that have been massaged to break down their tissues and reduce their salt content.

A culinary fact of life begins to take shape from all of this: in the world of food it is never safe to take anything for granted because often things are not as one assumes them to be on the basis of reasonability. How reasonable is the Jerusalem artichoke? It neither comes from Jerusalem nor is an artichoke; it comes from America and is a member of the sunflower family. The sea cucumber is not a plant nor is Bombay duck a fowl; both are edible marine animals. Headcheese is not cheese; it is the jellied meat from a pig's or a sheep's head. The banana is not a fruit; botanically speaking, the edible portion is classified as a berry while the plant itself is considered to be an herb, the tallest herb in the world. Onions, garlic, and asparagus are lilies, wild rice is a grass, the giant conch is a snail, the sweet potato is a morning glory, eggplants and chili peppers are cousins to deadly nightshade and narcotic mandrake, the horseshoe crab is kin to the spider, and peanuts are beans, not nuts.

Breadfruit itself doesn't even seem to know what it is. Starting out as the green-skinned, five-inch globular fruit of a South Pacific mulberry tree, when it is baked it tastes like wheat bread. However, as it ripens and begins to turn yellowish it becomes a vegetable tasting exactly like a yam. Then, when it is fully ripe and fully yellow it changes course once again, becoming a sweet dessert. But breadfruit, which was the cargo aboard H.M.S. *Bounty* when its crew mutinied against Captain Bligh, gives its identity crisis yet another twist by acting like a nut—its seeds are widely eaten because they taste like chestnuts.

Sauerkraut is not German; it is Chinese. It was eaten in China at least two hundred years before Christ and was brought to Europe by the Huns five hundred years after His death. The croissant—that delectable, crescent-shaped soft roll hailed as a gem of French baking—isn't French; it is Austrian and was brought to Paris from Vienna by Marie Antoinette in 1770. And, while we are at it, French fries are not French, they are Belgian. Swiss steak is not Swiss, Russian dressing is not Russian, English muffins are not English, and chop suey is not Chinese; all are American. Liederkranz, the cheese that sounds so German you can almost glimpse the barges on the Rhine, was created by a cheesemaker in Monroe, New York, in 1892. Vichyssoise, the soup that sounds as French as Liederkranz does German, was invented in the kitchens of New York City's Ritz-Carlton in 1910 (although a French chef employed at the hotel did have a major role in its invention).

It isn't always easy to ferret out the actual paternity of a particular food and sometimes to attempt it is to venture into an international minefield. The chauvinistic tug-of-war over the doughnut demonstrates the point. Food buffs in the United States firmly claim the doughnut as a gift from these shores to the taste-buds of humanity, tracing its genesis to the "fry bread" of the Indians. The Dutch say this is nonsense. "Every schoolchild knows that the Pilgrims spent eleven years in Holland before setting out to colonize America. How do you suppose they spent those years among us? Learning how to make our fried, sweet cakes, that's how. Then they crossed the Atlantic, fried our cakes, called them doughnuts, and added insult to injury by claiming that they were American."

This culinary dispute may never be resolved but at least the hole in the doughnut is unarguably American. The only question is which American merits recognition as the father of the hole. Technically, the honor goes to John Blondell who in 1872 was granted a U.S. patent for the world's first doughnut cutter that punched out a center hole. "Forget technicalities," urges the National Dunking Association. "A New England sea captain, Hanson Gregory, created the hole when he began cutting the centers out of the pastries in 1847 and a bronze plaque in his hometown, Rockport, Massachusetts, hails that inspired achievement."

Paradoxically, food chauvinists can argue just as resolutely to disclaim national responsibility for a specific dish as to claim it. More often than not, the target of this reverse chauvinism is American cuisine. One need look no farther than a bowl of chili con carne to find the proof. Despite its quite undeniable south-of-the-border accent, it is firmly, even aggressively disclaimed by Mexico. The Mexicans are more than merely content to retire from the field and leave Senators Goldwater and Tower to do battle for chili, they are anxious that the rest of the world recognize Mexico's noninvolvement in creation of the dish.

A frequently repeated allegation is that Americans have

sabotaged humanity's tastebuds by creating auto-
matic food-vending machines spewing out cellophane-
entombed sandwiches that are a culinary abomination.
The actual facts are a total vindication for America. The
mechanism for vending foods automatically was invented
in Sweden, and the cellophane was a Swiss invention. The
first food-vending machines in the United States, installed
in Philadelphia in 1902, were imported from Germany
where they were manufactured under license from the
Swedes. And the sandwich itself was invented in ancient
Rome and then was reinvented by the Earl of Sandwich in
London's Beefsteak Club in 1762. It is also appropriate to
note the role of the English in what they denounce as an
American sin for which no penance is great enough: the
serving of tea as an iced instead of a hot beverage as, they
insist, God intended it. The plain truth of the matter is
that iced tea is purely an English creation. It was devised
by an English employee of the Far East Tea House, a
British food pavilion at the 1904 St. Louis World's Fair.

As a last, seemingly defensible, fall-back position,
diehards cling to the belief that at the very least Americans
cannot evade responsibility for what food snobs dismiss as a
contemptible culinary impertinence: the lowly doggie
bag. As one might expect, criticism of the "American
doggie bag mentality" runs deep in France. After all, that
is where the first strawberries of spring and the first
walnuts of fall must be sent to the President of the Republic, and where every week for his seven years as first

President after World War II, Vincent Auriol required a restaurant four hundred miles distant to deliver to him in his official palace a big pot of its specialty: a casserole of beans, goose, and sausage. But it appears that it was actually in France, that shrine of those to whom eating is virtually a form of cult worship, that the doggie bag was invented.

The authoritative food historian, Roy Andries de Groot, reports that it was none other than the eminent nineteenth-century author and food fancier, Alexandre Dumas *pere,* who is responsible for the doggie bag. As de Groot explains it, Dumas was so accomplished a cook that invitations to his dinners were sought avidly. In the event that an invited guest could not attend because of an unbreakable prior engagement, all was not necessarily lost. The friend sent a servant over to Dumas's house and the remarkable master of pen and pot carefully bagged a portion of the evening's fare for the absent guest.

While the gurus of the kitchen seem to take delight in probing American cuisine for weaknesses, they have no hesitancy in pilfering its strengths, always making sure to cover their tracks by adopting subterfuges to draw a veil over their larceny. Consider what happened to that delectable bird that, if Benjamin Franklin had had his way, would have beaten out the bald eagle as America's feathered symbol. The English happily made room for the succulent bird in London's ovens but masked its birthplace by ignoring its original redskin name, instead calling it a turkey despite the fact that none had ever nested within sight of that country. Sowing similar geographic confusion, the Dutch called it the *kalkoen,* the Calcutta, while the Germans called it the Calcutta hen—*calecutischer Hahn*—though in time they repented sufficiently to rename it *Truthahn.* The French, bolder than their two neighbors, let the Dutch and the Germans have the city while they took over the whole country, dubbing the American creature the bird of India, *d'Inde,* later dropping the apostrophe to make it simply *dinde.*

When it defines food the dictionary turns out to be uncharacteristically inadequate, content to say merely that food is a nourishing substance taken into the body to sustain life. While that is true enough it is as meager a description as saying that Einstein was good at math. It has been clear ever since Adam and Eve did away with the apple—or with the pomegranate or banana, as the case may be—that food does much more than simply sustain life. It also quickens the spirit, invigorates the mind, and stimulates the imagination.

Chapter Two

BIAS IN THE COOKPOTS

All prejudices may be
tracked back to the intestines.

FRIEDRICH W. NIETZSCHE

ay what you will about prejudices, this much at least seems beyond dispute: when *we* have them they are perfectly reasonable and sensible but when *they* have them they are unreasonable and senseless. A surprisingly large number of prejudices—deeply held beliefs that either do or do not make sense, according to who is telling the story— relate to foods. It has been so since earliest times when people became convinced that this food or that was endowed with qualities influencing religion, sexual vigor, disease, or magic. Some of these beliefs, only a few, have withstood the tests of time and of broad public acceptance, or have survived the rigors of scientific proof. But all of them—the surviving beliefs as well as those that have been abandoned along the way—reveal the unique capacity of foods to generate myths and superstitions, to serve as symbols, and to arouse human emotions. Nothing illustrates the point more convincingly than the brashest and most exuberant member of the lily family: garlic.

There has never been a time when humanity ignored garlic, nor has there ever been an herb called upon to play more roles in more different ways. Many of the ancients held up garlic as a sacred food intertwined with their forms of worship. The Egyptians used it as a religious symbol and as an instrument for invoking their gods. When King Tut's tomb was discovered in 1922, more than 3,200 years after Egyptian priests had sealed it, it contained six bulbs of garlic that had been placed in it to speed the monarch on his rendezvous with the gods. Some early Hebrew sects used garlic in their marriage ceremonies as an augury of happiness for the wedded couple. In Greece garlic was used in temple ceremonies.

A persistent belief (subscribed to by some even in modern times) was that garlic had magic, supernatural powers. True believers of the herb's magic were never very difficult to spot—they were given away by the pungent odor of the garlic poultices they wore to ward off evil spirits or to assure themselves of long life, or both. Physical strength is something else that garlic was supposed to provide; Roman charioteers ate it by the handful for the power and endurance they expected it to bring them. Some among the faithful believed that garlic's ability to strengthen one included invigorating one's sexual performance.

Healers had a field day with garlic. Most of mankind's assorted ailments were at one time or another believed to melt away when confronted by the herb's curative capabilities. Among the ills supposedly vanquished by garlic were convulsions, plague, colds, hemorrhoids, influenza, and digestive problems. (There is some evidence that garlic does, in fact, aid in digestion.)

The most universally eaten vegetable, the onion, is a slightly less assertive member of the same family as garlic and has often been considered to do many of the same things as its more pushy cousin. Egyptians made a place for the onion in their religious ritual, using it as a temple decoration. They also esteemed it as a source of strength; the thousands of slaves who built the pyramids were fed a diet consisting largely of onions and garlic, which makes it clear that at the very least their breath was remarkably strong. The Romans looked on onions as an aphrodisiac, while healers in many lands prescribed them routinely as a specific against a variety of maladies. One staunch admirer of onions was George Washington, who ate them in great number. He wasn't sold on onions as a cure-all for his aches and pains or as a turn-on for a romp with Martha; he simply liked their flavor.

Where onions and garlic led, numerous herbs and spices followed. Rosemary was for centuries carried in funeral processions in Europe to ward off the forces of evil and bunches of it were buried with the dead for the same purpose; it was also dried and burned as ritual incense in religious ceremonies. The Egyptians used thyme to prepare their dead for burial; the Athenians used it to purify their temples and to treat poor vision and weak lungs. (Modern pharmacists often include thyme as an ingredient in their cough syrups.) In Greek mythology bay was associated with the gods and in Roman mythology the bay leaf symbolized triumph and wisdom; both the Greeks and the Romans credited it with holding off sorcerors, poisoners, epidemics, and liver ailments. In India basil occupies a position of prominence; considered to be sacred, it is—as in centuries past—planted around temples and burned on funeral pyres to accompany the soul to paradise.

The mushroom, the edible fungus that the ancients called "the plant without leaves," captured the attention of many peoples at least since the time of the Sumerians who were quite fond of it. Most of the ancients believed that the mushroom was magic fare, that it was created by bolts of lightning. Because ordinary citizens did not rate such magic food, in Egypt none but the pharaohs were permitted to eat it. The Romans, too, placed mushrooms in a class by themselves, considering them to be food of and for the gods, although that did not stop upper-class Romans from eating them. A species of mushroom found mainly in Mexico was long ago discovered to be hallucinogenic and its mind-altering capability led some to believe that it was sacred. Eating hallucinogenic mushrooms to create a trancelike state became a part of the religious ritual of some sects.

One of the oldest prepared foods, yogurt-type cheese, was popular among the Sumerians, the Chaldeans, and the Assyrians who considered it to be divinely inspired so that consuming it was almost in the nature of taking a sacrament. The Greeks, also believing it to be a gift of the gods, used it as a training diet for athletes preparing for the Olympic Games. The most dedicated yogurt enthusiast of modern times was Dr. Ilya Metchnikoff, co-winner of the 1908 Nobel Prize in Medicine and Physiology. He urged the eating of yogurt to slow the advance of the one disease certain to do us all in if we make it past all the other hazards: the aging process. What convinced Dr. Metchnikoff was his discovery that Bulgarians ate more yogurt and lived longer than other nationalities, attaining ages of one hundred and more in surprising numbers. From then on he ate the cheese unfailingly on a daily basis. Despite his high, consistent intake of yogurt he did not live beyond the threescore and ten that the Bible lays down as everyone's expectable life-span, whether or not one eats yogurt.

Among the fruits, apples seem regularly to have generated strong beliefs. For the Greeks and the Romans the apple was a symbol of marriage. Later the Celts also associated the apple with marriage. Then, more and more, the apple became the darling of the healers. A sixth-century medical text prescribes apples as a cure for diarrhea, but a fourteenth-century text does a 180-degree turn by citing them as a cure for constipation. One sixteenth-century physician asserted that when taken with milk, apples would cure anything. Other healers, a little more restrained if not necessarily any more accurate, spelled out the specific conditions that would flee when confronted by an apple; among them were indigestion, rheumatism, and warts. Even today many, especially those who grow the fruit commercially, like to tell us that an apple a day keeps the doctor away. What really keeps them away is that they have quit making house calls—apple-eaters have to see doctors as frequently as apple-abstainers.

In the Western Hemisphere corn more than any other

food was woven intricately into religious beliefs and customs of the Aztecs, the Incas, the Mayans, and the more northern Indians, all of whom believed it to be a divine food. At the start of each growing season the Inca emperor himself ritualistically planted the first seeds of the new crop. Temples dedicated to the corn deities were numerous in South America and at least one Inca temple was surrounded by a make-believe garden of corn plants fashioned from solid gold and silver; the remarkable garden was plundered by *conquistadores* greedy for riches to send back to Spain.

A second food that played a role in the spiritual life of the Western Hemisphere was the squash. Several Indian tribes used squash seeds in their religious rites. Often they also carved the shells into ritual masks. This last practice continues in modern America, shorn of its religious implications—it emerges each Halloween in the popular jack-o'-lanterns that are carved from pumpkins, a member of the squash family.

In the Far East chickens have long had a place in religious belief and frequently were sacrificed to appease the gods. The Chinese in particular perceived great spiritual powers behind those wings and drumsticks—they were convinced that a rooster's crowing at sunrise sent nocturnal ghosts fleeing and that its picture painted on a building protected the structure from fire. The Chinese also reserved a prominent place for the pig in their religious rites, offering it as a sacrifice to their gods. If the god being honored was one of the major deities, the pig was offered with its entrails hanging, considered a special mark of reverence. For the annual Festival of the Tombs the sacrificial pig was offered to the gods roasted, a tidier presentation than with innards trailing.

But if the pig has enjoyed—assuming being offered as a sacrifice can be enjoyable—an honored place in the religious rites of some it has been reviled and labeled a defilement by others. Both Jews and Moslems believe the pig is a foul animal and both religions place a ban on it. Interestingly, present-day Turkey—a Moslem country— is where the pig was first domesticated as a food animal 9,000 years ago.

Of all foods none has deeper, more significant links to religion than bread. For Christians, bread symbolizes the body of Christ; it plays a central role in the fundamental Christian sacrament of Holy Communion, while Christ Himself said, "I am the bread of life." And with just five loaves of bread, and two fish, Christ was miraculously able to feed the multitudes. For Jews, too, bread—in the form of matzoth, an unleavened bread—has major religious significance. It is eaten during Passover to symbolize the escape of the Jews from Egyptian bondage more than 3,000 years ago.

A reminder of the interplay between food and religion was provided in an unusual way recently when the U.S. Supreme Court let stand a decision by the Third Circuit Court of Appeals that has no precedent. The plaintiff in the case was a convicted felon serving time in the Pennsylvania state prison. He claimed to be a "naturalist minister" of a small sect and he asserted that the doctrine of his church prohibited the eating of any cooked foods. Charging that the authorities violated his religious rights every time they served him the normal prison diet, he sued to require that he be provided a special menu consisting entirely of raw foods. After evaluating all of the factors, the court determined that the sect was not a valid religion in a legal sense and therefore serving the plaintiff the regular prison diet was not a denial of his religious rights.

The Pennsylvania convict failed in his attempt to navigate a course around the prison cookpots but his suit did emphasize that what is perceived on the plate often depends on who is doing the looking. That is exactly the way it has been with ginseng. When today's "health food" enthusiasts look at it they perceive a root from which they can prepare a bracing tea. But two hundred years ago when Samuel Shaw, a canny Bostonian, looked at ginseng he perceived opportunity knocking on his door.

Shaw had heard that in the Orient ginseng was—as it still is—prized as an aphrodisiac and he intended to cash in on this belief in its ability to stoke up the human sexual furnace. So he loaded forty tons of the root aboard a sailing vessel, the *Empress of China,* and set his compass heading for the Far East. Six months later he dropped anchor in Canton, the first American trader ever to reach China. Disposing of his cargo for a princely sum, Shaw—and then other Americans—began a booming ginseng trade with

China. They scoffed at the Oriental belief in its aphrodisiacal effect but were happy to profit from it. As far as
the Americans were concerned, there was only one aphrodisiac that did the trick: oysters. Now it was the turn of
the Chinese to scoff because they were certain the shellfish
had quite the opposite effect on sexual drive. For centuries
Chinese pharmacologists had been cautioning against eating oysters after dark, warning that they were a sexual
turnoff. (Why anybody would ever have taken an oyster
seriously in matters related to sex is a mystery because the
creature itself is incapable of making up its own mind
about such things. A biological freak, it is a hermaphro-
dite, starting life sexless and then, as it matures, switching
back and forth from male to female, a zigzag it continues
throughout its lifetime.)

If Montezuma, the Aztec emperor, had still been alive
he would have been amused by the Americans with their
oysters and the Chinese with their ginseng because he was
certain that the only food that could be counted on to
deliver in the bedroom was chocolate. Before visiting his
very numerous harem he never failed to down a drink of
chocolate dissolved in water. It now appears that while
Montezuma was not necessarily aboard the right train he
was at least on the right track—modern chemical analysis
reveals that chocolate contains theobromine and caffeine,
both of them stimulants. Thus, while the chocolate may
have done little for his sexual vigor, at least it kept him
awake.

Ginseng, oysters, and chocolate are only the merest tip

of the aphrodisiacal iceberg on the pantry shelf; at some time or another almost everything that is edible has been thought to arouse passion and lust. The aromatic herb marjoram, supposedly first grown by Venus on Mount Olympus, was used by the ancients to concoct love potions, a custom that persisted as late as the nineteenth century in some parts of England, France, Italy, Greece, and Spain. Another herb, rosemary, was believed to stimulate lasting love; Romans wove it into bridal wreaths and newlyweds placed it beneath their mattresses. Throughout Europe both the purple eggplant and richly fragrant basil were considered surefire for arousing sensual love. The fourteenth-century Italian writer, Giovanni Boccaccio, penned a tale of basil growing from a pot watered by tears from Isabella who wept for her slain lover.

In classical Greece, eating a combination of carrots and leeks was thought to be a guarantee of sexual vigor. Chinese medical men during the T'ang Dynasty favored roast songbirds, but only during the winter months and only for males. The artichoke, said to have been created when a beautiful woman was turned into a thistle, was popular as an aphrodisiac in Elizabethan England where doctors prescribed them for patients seeking to pump up bedroom performance and where, in the slang of that era, a woman of easy morals was known as an artichoke. The French, long confident of their supremacy in matters related to either the bedroom or the kitchen, considered the artichoke to be only one of many weapons available in the arsenal of aphrodisiacs.

Madame de Maintenon, mistress of France's Louis XIV, had her own complex recipe for a dish to restore her sovereign's ardor; among its ingredients were veal, basil, coriander, cloves, anchovies, and brandy. Apparently the next royal playmate, Madame du Barry, had little confidence in Madame de Maintenon's recipe. She put her faith, as did a number of her countrymen, in ginger, regularly serving the new king, Louis XV, heavily gingered desserts.

It is left to present-day Indonesians to claim aphrodisiacal powers for the durian, an Asian fruit that would seem the least likely to stimulate thoughts of love. An encounter with a durian is no casual matter. Weighing as much as twenty pounds, this globe-shaped fruit encased in a prickly green rind has a stench that is overpoweringly repulsive. So foul-smelling is the durian that Asian airlines and railroads prohibit passengers from bringing it aboard. Those who praise the durian insist that if you can get past the stench to sink your teeth in it the creamy pulp is an enjoyable reward for your courage.

Indonesian faith in the durian's capacity to serve above and beyond a fruit's normal duty demonstrates that food has not lost its power to grip the human imagination. This was again confirmed in a recent report in the medical press. According to the account a French professor of obstetrics has announced that by controlling the diet of a couple during the six weeks prior to conception he has achieved an 88 percent success rate in enabling them to produce a baby of the sex they wish. To produce a male baby the obstetrician places the couple on a diet of meat, bananas, peaches, beans, and artichokes while he bans all dairy foods and eggs. To produce a girl he withholds coffee, ham, sausage, and most cheeses, and instead prescribes mostly vegetables and fruits. The emphasis on fruits would be welcomed by an Indonesian couple wanting a female baby—they could concentrate on those durians.

Chapter Three

SECOND HELPINGS, ANYONE?

What is food to one man
may be fierce poison to others.

LUCRETIUS

f, somehow, Lucretius were to be restored to life today—2,000 years after he offered his observation in Rome—he would undoubtedly point to Japan and say, "See, what did I tell you?" What Lucretius would be drawing attention to is a kind of dinner-table Russian roulette the Japanese play, using a blowfish instead of a revolver as their weapon. The blowfish is, in a most literal sense, poison. It becomes edible only if before it is cooked someone who really knows his business carefully and completely removes its liver and ovaries, the organs containing its poison.

Somehow, it is not terribly surprising that a country able to produce World War II's Kamikaze pilots would not be put off by a hazard like poison. So the Japanese, considering the flavor of the creature to outweigh its risk, eat blowfish. Unfortunately for a number of them each year, the blowfish becomes their last meal on earth.

If it is logic you are looking for don't seek it in the world of food. On one hand are people who willingly, even enthusiastically, risk poisoning at the dinner table. On the other hand are people who, fearful of being poisoned, shun some foods long after they have been demonstrated to be completely harmless. The workhorse vegetable of the West, the potato, was discovered by European explorers in 1534 in South America where it had long been an established, nourishing feature of the local diet. Despite all the evidence to the contrary, Europeans for a long time feared potatoes, fully convinced that they were harmful. Legislators in France, believing potatoes could cause leprosy, went so far as to issue an edict banning their cultivation. Germany permitted a loophole in its defenses against the potato; cultivation was limited, until almost the beginning of the nineteenth century, to producing food for pigs and for jailed convicts.

Many Americans shared this irrational fear of potatoes. Even as late as the early 1900s some Americans were completely convinced that the only way a potato could be prepared safely for the table was to boil it first for a lengthy period to leach out the poisons it contained. An American cookbook published in 1904 warned against reuse of the water in which potatoes had been boiled because it has "been known to poison a dog."

To a modern generation hooked on French fries and potato chips condemnation of the potato as a health hazard is ludicrous if not actually an act of hostility. But it is no more ludicrous than the fear of fresh fruit that once gripped a large segment of the nation. In 1830 a New York newspaper warned that fresh fruits were a health hazard, especially for children. The Chicago press went further, calling on the city council to ban the sale of fresh fruit because it caused cholera. One paper carried a lurid account of two boys who supposedly ate oranges and coconut with the tragic result that "one was a corpse and the other was reduced to the last stage of cholera."

And then there is the tomato. Like the potato, it is native to South America, was introduced into Europe by sixteenth-century explorers, and was promptly dismissed as poisonous despite the evidence of its safe consumption in its original home. For two centuries Europeans shunned the tomato. At last Italians screwed up their courage and began modest, experimental introduction of tomatoes into their cooking. The results were a culinary success unblemished by death, disease, or even mild discomfort. Encouraged, more and more Italians began eating tomatoes and Italy's farmers, responsive to the growing marketplace demand, worked at developing improved strains of the plant.

Hearing of the Italian success with tomatoes, Thomas Jefferson—always the innovator on his Virginia farm—planted them as a food crop in 1781, the very first American to do so. Though Jefferson ate tomatoes enthusiastically and sang their praises loudly, almost no one raised a voice in harmony. His countrymen were willing enough to acknowledge his bravery in eating tomatoes, or his foolhardiness as some would put it, but they shared Europe's general fear of them and few would join him. Most Americans remained skeptical of the tomato until well into the nineteenth century. Paradoxically, a few health fanatics and healers had begun some years earlier to tout the tomato as a remedy for indigestion, liver ailments, and diarrhea and as a protection against cholera. One huckster began bottling a cure-all labeled as Dr. Miles's Compound Extract of Tomato. It may have done little good but it seems not to have done any harm.

If a streak of contrariness is a part of the American character, food serves to emphasize it. These same Americans who were for a long time fearful of some foods were often quite adventurous in entrusting their digestive tracts to others that would arouse little enthusiasm—or even mere acceptance—among their modern countrymen. They were seldom reluctant to eat wildcat, beaver tail, raccoon, muskrat, opossum, porcupine liver, moose nose, coot, and bear. Bear was favored because its meat provided dinner while its fat rendered a double-barreled service as cooking oil and as hair dressing. Mark Twain got into the spirit when he observed, "In the matter of diet I have always been persistently strict in sticking to things which didn't agree with me until one or the other of us got the best of it."

Americans, in their willingness to eat much that strikes many today as unappealing, perhaps even repulsive, were only demonstrating—though on a less lethal plane—the same universal truth as the Japanese with their blowfish: what sounds like a dinner bell to some often sounds like a warning buzzer to others. Which way it will turn out—mealtime turn-on or mealtime turnoff—is a matter of perceptions, attitudes, and conditioning.

When it came to food, the wealthy of ancient Rome had tastes that were, to be charitable about it, imaginative. Among the foods that occupied places of prominence at their banquets were cows' udders, sea nettles, cranes, flamingos, birds' tongues and birds' brains, and dormice. The dormice were fattened for the table in special containers—the fatter the rodents, the more honor the host was rendering to his guests.

Athenians enjoyed roasted insects of several varieties. The Bible itself enumerates, in Leviticus, the insects that it is permissible to eat: locusts, beetles, and grasshoppers. Vietnamese royalty of centuries past were more attuned to creatures considerably larger than insects. They graced their table with such tasties as elephant, rhinoceros, peacock pie, and orangutan lips.

The passage of time since dormice, cows' udders, and orangutan lips were in style has done little to tame or inhibit the unpredictable, freewheeling human tastebud. Some of the old dinner-table favorites may have disappeared but they have been replaced by new ones equally bizarre or equally delicious, depending on whose plate they land on. Queen Elizabeth learned this—reluctantly—on a recent visit to a British Commonwealth outpost: Tuvalu, in the South Pacific. The Tuvaluans feted their queen with a feast featuring blackbird stew and roast bats.

A Russian delicacy, hard to come by these days, is bears' paws, while in northern Italy it is smoked donkey that is highly esteemed. Spaniards enjoy barnacles, a leading contender for the title of world's ugliest marine animal, and among some Spanish peasants a favored dish is cat poached in sherry. Ant eggs and stuffed frogs rate highly in Laos, as does *padek,* a sauce made of bits of fermented fish smelling so strong that the saucepot is kept outdoors. In Belgium a dish made with hare's blood draws praise, but on the other side of the world in Bali it is one made with turtle's blood. A Singapore specialty is curried fish head. The Burmese enjoy a salad of pickled tea leaves. Australians dote on kangaroo tail, while the Aborigines in the back country favor roast lizard. A popular food in Central America is iguana, and in the Seychelles it is flying fox, a batlike creature. Snake is esteemed in Hong Kong, not only for its flavor but also for its supposed relief of rheumatism. Modern technology has rendered a service to the snake-eaters of Hong Kong: markets there have begun offering packaged instant snake soup.

Visitors from Hong Kong would feel comfortable in an American-owned restaurant in Brussels that serves rattlesnake and, when it is able to arrange for supplies, boa constrictor. Other offerings on the menu include ostrich, monkey, and alligator. In Paris, Paul Corcellet's food shop offers python, elephant trunk, and crocodile; hardly the sort of place one dashes into for a half-pound of cheese and some dill pickles. Even Dallmayr's in Munich, a luxurious German food emporium where Mozart used to drop in for some of its specialties whenever the eighteenth-century musical genius was in town, includes sea gull eggs, roast pigs' heads, and smoked bears' hams among its thousands of offerings.

One visits Washington's celebrated Smithsonian Institution expecting to confront the unusual but fully confident that one will be expected only to admire it, not to consume it. Such confidence may be unsafe, as guests at a recent Smithsonian reception discovered. Passed around among the guests were platters of attractive cookies—baked of ground-up mealworms. There was a certain appropriateness about the unconventional offering since the occasion marked the fifth anniversary of the Institution's Insect Zoo. Nevertheless, many of the guests experienced no difficulty in restraining their enthusiasm for eating the cookies. However, in much of the modern world insects of all kinds are a large and welcome part of the human diet. (It could also be pointed out that Americans are unwitting consumers of insects. Under the U.S. Food and Drug Administration regulations food processors are permitted to reach specified—and harmless—levels of insect infestation in the products they turn out for public sale. Thus, canned mushrooms may contain up to 20 maggots per 100 grams but tomato paste is limited to two maggots per 100 grams. Raisins may include up to 10 insects and 35 fly eggs per eight ounces. Apple butter may contain unlimited quantities of aphids, mites, and thrips.)

In Australia a lemonade-like drink is made from green weaver ants, while sugar ants are considered by some

Aussies to be a toothsome delicacy. White ants are eaten in Brazil and in Sweden some whiskies are distilled with ants added for flavoring. The modern world's costliest and rarest food flavoring is Ca Cuong, a secretion the Vietnamese obtain from beetles. In many parts of Africa termites are a favored dish, said by fans to taste like pineapple. They also caution that one should not dawdle when eating live termites because if given half a chance the creatures will beat the diner to the first bite.

Dragonflies are a popular food in parts of East Africa, frequently sauteed with onions. Other dinner-table insects include praying mantis, palm weevil grubs, beetles, bees, locusts, crickets, caterpillars, silkworms, moth larvae, and maguey worms. But probably the most universally eaten insect is the grasshopper, which seems a highly appropriate way for getting back at it for being such a destructive insect. Grasshoppers are served in several different forms: toasted, fried, boiled, ground, dried, and salted. Nutritionists like to point out that the grasshopper is an impressive 60 percent protein while cooked beef is only 29 percent protein.

Despite the wide acceptance elsewhere of insects as food suitable for humans, and despite FDA's permissive attitude on introducing the creatures into the American digestive tract, the nation continues to be repulsed by the thought of eating them. Perhaps this repulsion would diminish somewhat if the creatures were referred to not as insects but as arthropods, which is their scientific classification. (A few years ago when commercial fishermen could find no market for dogfish they very astutely fileted the fish and offered the filets as "ocean perch," and now they sell all they can catch. When the Danes refused to buy catfish, markets in Denmark labeled it "cutlet fish" and found willing buyers.) It isn't as though Americans don't already eat certain arthropods. In fact, they happily pay premium prices for the arthropods that they esteem, although they call for them by the familiar names of lobster, shrimp, and crab.

One can always call a spade a spade with the Chinese; it requires no subterfuge or linguistic camouflage like calling an insect an arthropod to lure them to the dinner table. Dr. Lin Yutang, the famed Chinese author and philospher, once said, only half-jokingly, "If there is anything we Chinese are serious about, it is neither religion or learning, but food. We openly acclaim eating as one of the few joys of this human life."

Of all peoples, the Chinese are probably the world's least inhibited, most adventurous eaters. True culinary free spirits, their cookpots welcome almost anything that lives on land or in the sea or in the air—from dog to frog, from pig's ear to shark's fin, from jellyfish to sparrow to seaweed to grasshopper. And once something winds up in a Chinese cookpot it can count on being prepared for table in ways that are original, imaginative and—often—quite surprisingly unconventional. Consider what happens to fowl.

The Chinese are willing enough to do to a chicken what

others elsewhere do—frying, roasting, stewing, barbecuing, and the other familiar routines—but they also have a way of looking at a chicken and seeing possibilities that nobody else spotted. They smoke chicken in tea, bake it in clay, slow-cook it imbedded in salt, shred it, steam it, dry it in the sun. They prepare dishes from the chicken's head, from its feet, from its intestines, or from its blood. One of their specialties is a dish prepared from cocks' combs. Not always content to wait for the chicken to hatch, they also do considerable culinary freewheeling with the egg— including pickling, steaming, smoking, and salt-curing eggs. But they pull out all the stops when they turn their attention to preparing their thousand-year-old eggs.

The first thing to understand about a thousand-year-old egg is that it isn't. It may look that old to some and may taste that old to others but it is actually only two or three months old. To prepare this delicacy the Chinese use duck eggs. They start off by coating the eggs with a thick mix of lime, pine ash, and salt. Then they pack mud around the eggs, roll them in straw until they adhere to the mud lushly, and bury them in the ground to ferment. Anywhere from sixty to ninety days later they are dug up. By now the eggs have taken on a brownish hue and almost jellylike consistency, and have absorbed through their shells an earthy, metallic flavor from their various coatings. They are now judged to be a delicious morsel by those who find merit in that sort of thing.

The Chinese also used to cook eggs by lowering them in the shell into natural hot springs containing a very high sulfur content. Allowed to remain in the springs for several hours, the eggs absorbed a strong taste and odor of sulfur. This method of cooking dwindled away about a thousand years ago. It is difficult to believe that anyone mourned its passing.

Whatever one feels about the end product, surely one must salute the Chinese for their originality and daring in the kitchen. But after their razzle-dazzle in bringing fowl and eggs to the table along pathways untrodden by others, what can the Chinese do for an encore? One thing they can, and do, do is to evict the fowl from its home and then eat its vacated nest. Not just any nest will serve this purpose—it must be from a swift that makes its home on the edge of the South China Sea. Chinese who are expert in all matters related to bird's nest soup, divide the nests into two separate quality grades: white and black. The white nest, the one prized most highly by the connoisseurs, is made by the swift entirely from saliva it secretes. The black nest, only a little less delicious in the view of its fans, is composed of the swift's saliva plus bits of seaweed it has gathered and tiny feathers it has shed.

Westerners tempted to shake their heads in bafflement over the poor Chinese who will go so far as to eat bird spit ought to heed the admonition about people in glass houses throwing stones. The fact is that the sticky, sweet stuff so popular in the West—honey—is actually matter that has been regurgitated by the bees. So East may be East and West may be West but when it comes to the birds and the bees the twain seem to have met on common ground.

Chapter Four

THE GOOD GUYS
WEAR WHITE HATS

Cookery is become an art,
a noble science;
cooks are gentlemen.

ROBERT BURTON

lthough much of the reign of King Assur-bani-pal of Assyria was turbulent with wars and with unrest, he did not let the turbulence divert him from encouraging the arts within his realm, including the culinary arts. Beating the Pillsbury company to its "bake-offs" by more than 2,600 years, Assur-bani-pal sponsored cooking contests and rewarded the winners with purses of gold.

Confucius, the great sage upon whose teachings rests one of the world's major religions, sought perfection in all things, including matters relating to the dinner table. Among his teachings are numerous instructions for the ideal methods of preparing and serving a wide variety of foods.

The noted statesman and reformer of ancient Rome, Cato, was a man of influence and of multiple interests. In his time he played a leading role in shaping the composition of the Roman senate, the nature of public works projects, the standards of public morality, and the way Romans treated a ham. Included among his surviving writings is a book that offers this advice on how to make a ham achieve maximum succulence: cure it in salt for seventeen days, dry it in the open air for two days, sponge the salt off and coat the ham with oil, smoke it for two days, coat it again with oil—this time mixed with vinegar—and then hang the ham in a cool place to mellow.

To Pope Pius V food was not a subject to be dismissed lightly. He established the character and standards of the Papal kitchens and then insisted that the staff adhere to them. His head cook, Bartolomeo Scappi, took the lid off the cookpot in 1570 with his book, *Cooking Secrets of Pope Pius V,* describing the Pope's menus, recipes, and dinner-table etiquette. One of Pius's banquets, as reported by Scappi, consisted of soup, stew, seven kinds of fowl, rabbit, goat, veal, beef and pork in several different ways, sweetbreads, liver, vegetables, pastries, fruits, nuts, wines and, as a final gesture of hospitality, toothpicks. (Leo XI, who succeeded Pius in 1605, died of overeating only twenty-five days after he was elevated to the Papal throne.)

A contemporary of Pope Pius's who had earned a rep-utation for indulging his stomach voluptuously was Henry VIII, King of England. So pleased was Henry one day by a pudding his chef prepared for him that he rewarded the man with the gift of a manor house, making it the most valuable pudding in history. Even the English penal sys-tem during Henry's regime reflected sympathy for those who catered to the stomach—the fine for killing a baker was three times greater than the fine for killing an ordinary citizen.

Almost the first act of George Washington after he was inaugurated as President of the brand-new United States was to compose a newspaper advertisement. This is how it read: "A cook is wanted for the family of the President of the United States. No one need apply who is not perfect in

the business and can bring indubitable testimonials of
sobriety, honesty, and attention to the duties of the station." Many days and many interviews later the President
finally found his man.

There is a point to all these incidents spanning the
centuries and the continents. The point is this: time and
geography, religion and politics, language and culture
may separate people from one another, but gastronomy—
the art of good eating—can link them. That is not to say
that all gastronomes march in step with one another behind the same culinary drummer. But all are at least
headed in the same direction. The gourmet moves along
leveling vigilant attention on the artistry, the delicacy,
and the quality of the table (though when the term first
came into use in France gourmet simply meant a wine
merchant). The gourmand appreciates quality and artistry
in a culinary performance but he also sets great store on
abundance, often excessively greedy abundance. It isn't
important that gastronomes may not themselves do the
cooking; what is important is that they understand and
applaud the talents of those who cook well and they savor
the delights the cooks set before them.

How dedicated to gastronomy one may become can be
gleaned from the case of Apicius, wealthy citizen of first-
century Rome and inventor of *pâté de foie gras*, the rich liver
paste that is mistakenly credited by almost everyone as
France's gift to gourmets everywhere. (He is also said by
some to have written the world's first proper cookbook, *De*

Re Coquinaria, but this is hardly likely since it appeared some two hundred years after he got up from the table for the last time.) All Rome schemed to be invited to dine with Apicius because his banquets were superbly, dazzlingly sumptuous. He offered his guests only the finest, freshest, most luxurious foods, prepared exquisitely by a remarkably skilled staff and served with flawless elegance. Eventually these tremendous extravagances became such a financial drain that Apicius realized he could no longer sustain the burden. Lowering his lofty standards to a level that he could support was unthinkable to him, so Apicius did what he considered to be the only honorable alternative for a true gourmet—he committed suicide.

Powerful though its grasp can be, seldom does gastronomy exert so strong a grip as to be terminal as it was for Apicius. If gastronomy does do anyone in it is usually because the victim vulgarized its principles and strayed from the high road of the gourmet into the quicksand of the glutton.

In Apicius' Rome there was no shortage of ostentatious gluttons gorging themselves toward an early grave. Digestive ailments, gout, liver trouble, ulcers, and obesity were common. One greedy emperor, Claudius I, one day consumed an enormous meal—dish after dish of fish, fowl, and meats prepared in many different ways. After he had done away with the last of this huge meal he still coveted some mushrooms and he believed that he could somehow find a way to shoehorn them into his bloated stomach. So

Claudius ordered his servants to fetch him a bowl of mushrooms. He ate them all and promptly died of acute indigestion. Aulus Vitellius, first-century Roman emperor noted equally for his dissipation and his incompetence, is alleged to have once eaten an astounding one thousand oysters at one sitting. Another emperor, Caligula, drank pearls dissolved in vinegar to make clear to everyone that nothing was too lavish or too precious for his table. Cleopatra once dissolved and consumed a mammoth pearl weighing 74 carats.

(Extreme ostentation has not yet disappeared from the consumption of food. In 1975 Craig Claiborne, food editor of *The New York Times,* and a friend sat down to dinner in a Paris restaurant, Chez Denis. Claiborne had worked out all the details with the establishment well in advance of their arrival, so as soon as they were comfortable the dishes began to come. And come. And come. Claiborne and his friend worked their way through a staggering thirty-one separate courses, pausing en route to sip nine different wines. The bill for that food orgy was equally staggering: $4,000, tax and tip included. The bill didn't bother Claiborne since American Express was paying it as a publicity stunt.)

If the dinner table turned out to be a trap for some Romans, it turned out to be an escape route for some Greeks. It happened during Greece's Byzantine period about 1,500 years ago when a number of intellectuals, having been singled out for harassment by an oppressive administration, sought refuge in Greece's many monasteries. Intellectuality and gastronomy often go hand in hand, so most of those who fled to the monasteries were quite at home in the kitchen. Thus, it seemed perfectly natural to them to volunteer to earn their keep by cooking for the monks. To distinguish them from the monks, all of whom wore tall black hats as a part of the religious garb, the new monastery cooks began to wear tall white hats. It was this tall white hat that would, in time, become recognized universally as the proud symbol of the professional chef.

At the same time that Byzantine repression was turning Greece's most cultured citizens into refugees within their own country, the Roman empire—weakened by all of its excesses—was disintegrating. Fragmented, feudalistic, rent by tribal warfare, Europe was now entering its twilight period: the Middle Ages that would for centuries see a stagnation of Western civilization. Except for a few isolated religious communities where scholarship and culture were still kept alive, often barely, this was a bleak time for intellectuality and for such civilizing influences as gastronomy.

Eating—dining was too fine a term for it—was now almost everywhere in Europe an exercise in crudeness. Quality had made way for quantity. On all sides there was gluttony, always excepting the poor for whom hunger was more usual. An acid-tongued ambassador from Naples, dispatched to France, looked about at the gluttony and hunger that existed side by side and observed that "Nine-tenths of the people die of hunger, one-tenth of indigestion."

It was in the fifteenth century that culinary refinement and restraint began to reappear in Europe and the resurgence came first in Italy. The rest of the continent continued to remain very largely a gastronomic wasteland. Then in the sixteenth century came an event that proved to be a culinary turning point for Europe: the arrival in France of Catherine de' Medici from her native Italy to become the wife of the Duke of Orléans. Catherine had the instincts of a true gourmet. But even more important, she brought with her from Italy a staff of highly skilled cooks and bakers.

The dishes that Catherine's kitchen retinue turned out created a stir in France's royal circles, producing a growing awareness that there was an alternative to the crudeness and heaviness of French food. Later, when the Duke of Orléans ascended to the throne as Henry II, Catherine—now the queen—exerted a profound influence over French culinary standards. This was the point at which France, learning from Italy and prodded by its Italian queen, began its climb toward gastronomic greatness. (This was not the first time that French cuisine was influenced by Italy. When Julius Caesar and his Roman legions invaded 2,000 years ago they brought with them stocks of one of their favorite foods: snails. Later generations would know the little creatures as the most French of French foods whereas it really is the most French of Italian foods.)

Another significant milestone along the culinary road came in 1775 when Anthelme Brillat-Savarin was born in the singularly aptly named French town of Belley. It was a droll accident of geographic nomenclature because Brillat-Savarin's belly would earn for him an enduring position of eminence among the heroes of gastronomy.

From his earliest years it was clear that Brillat-Savarin was endowed with a remarkable multiplicity of talents. He became a linguist fluent in a dozen languages, a lawyer, a chemist, and a teacher of law and chemistry at the University of Dijon. He invented the perfume atomizer, wrote works on economy, and became mayor of Belley after the French Revolution began. When the Revolution deteriorated into the bloody excesses of the Reign of Terror he fled to New York where for two years he supported himself by playing the violin in a theater orchestra. Returning home in 1797, Brillat-Savarin reestablished a law practice. A short time later he was appointed a judge and then commenced a rapid rise through the judicial ranks until he occupied a seat on France's highest court of appeals. But if he was linguist, inventor, lawyer, chemist, teacher, politician, musician, and judge, he permitted none of these pursuits to interfere with his two abiding passions: food and women. In his affairs of the heart he may have been fickle; in his affairs of the belly he was never casual.

For Brillat-Savarin food was not only the supreme pleasure of his life, it was also the focus of his intellectual curiosity. How, he wanted to know, does food affect emotions? What are the psychological and sociological implications of eating? How does taste function and how does it influence human behavior? What is the chemistry of obesity? Throughout his life he pondered these and other related questions, slowly shaping answers that satisfied his brilliant, questing mind. Then he devoted thirty years to writing, polishing, and refining his monumental *Physiologie du Gout—Physiology of Taste*—a work that encompassed his encyclopedic knowledge of food and reflected his profound adoration of the table. It was instantly hailed as the foremost work on gastronomy ever written. One critic proclaimed enthusiastically that the book brought the "flame of genius to the art of dining." Others echoed the same extravagant praise. Unfortunately for Brillat-Savarin, he had little time to enjoy his tremendous success. Only six weeks after publication of his landmark work in 1825, he was dead at the age of seventy-one. It is unlikely that the cemetery ever received a corpse possessed of a more distinguished belly and brain.

(Brillat-Savarin's passionate devotion to the pleasures of the table rubbed off on his sister, Pierrette. One evening when she was just two months shy of her one-hundredth birthday, and was confined to her bed because she was weak and was failing fast, she was nevertheless able to enjoy the dinner her servant had arranged on a tray on her lap. As she was finishing the main course she suddenly realized that death was only moments away. Crying out to her servant, she ordered, "Quick, bring me the dessert!" Alas, she breathed her last before it could be placed on her tray. One can only hope that a luscious dessert was awaiting Pierrette at the Pearly Gates.)

In the annals of gastronomy there are few whose names are worthy of being mentioned in the same sentence as Brillat-Savarin's. One of those chosen few is a countryman of his, Marie-Antoine Carême. Just as Brillat-Savarin has been hailed for having brought the "flame of genius to the art of dining" so must Carême be acknowledged for having brought the flame of genius to the art of cooking.

As the sixteenth child born into a desperately poor family (reportedly, his parents had nine more children after him) Carême knew almost from the beginning that it would be up to him to find his own way in life. What he could not anticipate was that he would have to find it so soon or so completely. When he was only eleven, in 1795, his father turned him out into the street to fend for himself. Fate was for once kind to him—he quickly found work in a pastry shop. Anxious to please his employer, Carême was a cheerfully energetic worker, fetching and carrying, washing and scrubbing, and willingly performing any other chore that came up. All the while, however, he kept one eye on the bakers to learn everything he could of the pastry-maker's art. Then, when he was in his late teens, he managed to have himself taken on as an apprentice chef. Again luck was with him because he worked under a succession of skilled master chefs, learning something worthwhile from each of them according to their strengths. By the time Carême reached his mid-twenties he was thoroughly schooled in all aspects of food preparation and was beginning to show the kind of culinary innovation and imagination that attracted attention among gourmets.

Talleyrand, the French foreign minister and a man who enjoyed the pleasures of the table as much as the intrigues of international diplomacy, was one of those who took note of Carême and he did something about it—he hired him as his personal chef. Inspired by Talleyrand's position and gastronomic sophistication and stimulated by the eminence of his employer's dinner guests, Carême flourished. He was not only masterful in preparing all of the classical dishes but he also displayed innovative flair in creating new ones of intricate complexity and superlative flavor. His desserts, especially, were unsurpassed; shaped, molded, and carved with artistry, they were actually beautiful sculptures that were a treat for eye as well as tongue.

The notables of Europe envied the French foreign minister his brilliant chef and tried to lure him into their own employ. After resisting the enticements as long as he could, Carême finally succumbed, embarking on a splendid and unprecedented procession from palace to palace, lingering in each long enough to bestow on it his special brand of culinary magic. He went to Vienna to cook for the Austrian emperor, to England to cook for the future King

George IV, to Russia to cook for Czar Alexander I, and then back to France where he served first as the chef for Baron Rothschild and then as chef for King Louis XIII himself. As a gourmet, Talleyrand missed Carême sorely, but as the French foreign minister he was delighted that his former chef moved in such exalted circles. Moving about freely in the kitchens and dining salons of Europe's crowned heads, treated with deference and respect, Carême was in a unique position to overhear much that could be useful intelligence. Remaining grateful and loyal to Talleyrand although now in the employ of others, Carême always passed on to the foreign minister all of the information that he picked up.

Whether or not Carême's intelligence reports had much influence on shaping French foreign policy decisions is unknown, but there is no guesswork about his effect on gastronomy—it was profound. He discovered new delicacies on his travels and brought them into the mainstream of gastronomy; among his discoveries were caviar and cheesecake. He himself created many notable dishes, including that delectable dessert, charlotte russe. But his most significant contribution was undoubtedly the many books he wrote. Intended primarily for professional chefs, they brought coherence, harmony, and order to cooking. In his books were hundreds of carefully detailed recipes (one recipe alone was seven pages long), and complete menus for all purposes and all occasions (one gala banquet menu consisted of an amazing forty-eight courses). They also contained instructions for decorating and serving all of the classical dishes and hundreds of lesser-known dishes, and even had detailed sketches showing how to sculpt his marvelous desserts. What he did, in effect, was to synchronize, interpret, adapt, and record the entire body of knowledge of early nineteenth-century European gastronomy.

When Marie-Antoine Carême died in 1833 he was mourned by the entire culinary world as "the king of cooks and the cook of kings." It was not linguistic overkill.

There is this to be said about true gastronomes: their quest for the pleasures of the table is constant, resolute, and resourceful. Commodore David G. Farragut, U.S. Navy, exemplifies what that means. In the fall of 1854 when the Navy Department ordered Farragut to northern California to establish a new naval base on Mare Island, he knew what he was letting himself in for. It would be a demanding, challenging mission because the small island was desolate, inhospitable, totally undeveloped. Everything would have to be barged out from the mainland: equipment and machinery, building materials, tools and supplies of every description, tents, work animals. Labor crews would have to live under crude field conditions while they went about the business of transforming a wilderness into an orderly, efficient base. Farragut understood all of this quite well and as a professional officer it did not dismay him. But Commodore Farragut was also a gastronome and as such he was dismayed that his mission would condemn him to a culinary purgatory unless he took decisive steps promptly to forestall that dreaded consequence.

Being the senior naval officer in the West gave Farragut considerable room to maneuver and he made the most of it. First, he secured a U.S. Navy sloop for his personal use. Next, he had the sloop fitted out with a private galley that would be properly ungrudging to the gastronome within him. Then he stocked his private galley with foods he deemed suitably responsive to his needs; among them were two barrels of dried Louisiana shrimps, forty smoked Virginia hams, one smoked pig of good size, five large canisters of Chilean beef marinated in red wine, and two whole sides of barbecued beef. Now that he deemed himself properly equipped to face the rigors of Mare Island, Farragut sailed there and anchored the sloop to serve as his personal command post and his gastronomic oasis in a culinary wasteland. He knew he could count on the nearby waters to supply his pantry with sturgeon, salmon, and other tasty fish and he expected to bag venison, quail, and other small game on the island itself. By the time he was finished with Mare Island he had succeeded in carving a fine base from it. He had, at the same time, managed to dine with the flair and the elegance that any gourmet would cherish. Given Farragut's enterprise and initiative, it is not surprising that he went on to become the U.S. Navy's first four-star admiral.

In the modern world—confronted so persistently by

canned goods whose labels read like chemical inventories, and by restaurants that too often promise more than they are capable of delivering—it may be difficult to realize that gastronomy is still alive and thriving. There are still those who pursue, with diligence and sensitivity, the art of preparing, serving, and enjoying fine food. Like the chef of a highly regarded French restaurant who was so anguished when the 1967 edition of the *Guide Michelin,* France's culinary bible, downgraded its rating of his kitchen performance that he shot himself. Apicius would have applauded. Brillat-Savarin and Carême would have understood. And Farragut would have saluted.

Chapter Five

THE FORTY-FOOT PICKLE AND OTHER EXTRAVAGANCES

. . . a man hath no better thing
under the sun than to eat, and
to drink, and to be merry.

ECCLESIASTES 8:15

istory of a sort was made one evening in 1900 when a switch was flipped at a downtown New York building to light up the city's very first, rooftop, electric advertising sign. This forerunner of the marketing spectaculars that would come along later was illuminated by 1,200 electric bulbs, a huge number in the statistics of that time. And what was displayed so blindingly by the 1,200 bulbs on New York's pioneering sign? A pickle, that's what, a forty-foot-long, crisp-and-crunchy-looking, green pickle that H. J. Heinz hoped would send passersby flocking to groceries to ask for by brand-name.

In surrounding his pickle with some of the glitter and pizzazz of show business Mr. Heinz was following a well-established tradition that couples food and spectacle for special occasions. It is a coupling that has had its moments of extravagant, even startling theatrics. Among the earliest and most notorious of them were those staged by Nero, the Roman emperor who made immorality his full-time pursuit.

A man of insatiable appetites—for food, for spectacle, for lusty and often perverted sex—Nero had no patience with moderation, restraint, or just plain good taste. The banquets he staged so frequently reflected all of the character flaws of the host. The food—course after course, each in huge quantity—consisted of exotic, expensive offerings, many of them carried to Rome from far distant lands. The food was not merely brought to the table, it was choreographed to the table. The servers, scantily clad girls and boys, danced to the table with their platters, their movements carefully synchronized with orchestral music. Once they had placed the platters on the tables the dancers gave themselves over to an inventively provocative and abandoned performance calculated to stimulate lust among the diners.

Nero had a thing about ceilings—he could not stand not to make them part of the show. In his largest banquet hall he had the ceiling constructed in such a way that at his signal it would roll back completely to permit slaves to swirl a gentle rain of scented flowers down over the guests. In a slightly smaller dining salon Nero had the ceiling—domed and painted to resemble the sky—cleverly engineered in such a way that it revolved steadily throughout the meal.

The most spectacular party Nero is supposed to have given is the one in which he is said to have fiddled while Rome burned behind him. It makes a good enough story but it is flawed. The fire, lasting for nine days and destroying two-thirds of the city, was real enough. But Nero, who took his music seriously and frequently entertained his guests by playing the flute, the harp, and pipes, and the lyre could not possibly have played the fiddle—it was not invented until some 1,500 years after he died. However, if the description of his alleged party does not hold up, it does seem nevertheless that he may have been an arsonist. Several of his contemporaries wrote at the time that Nero had Rome burned deliberately to clear vast areas for new construction he planned.

Of all of the couplings of food and spectacle probably none was ever more strangely ghoulish than the nightly banquets of the Prince de Condé in the last years of his life in seventeenth-century France. Having become mentally unbalanced, the prince one day announced to his palace staff that they were no longer to prepare meals for him because he had died and it was quite clear to everyone that a dead man could not eat. His alarmed major domo, unable to cope with the unique situation, at once summoned the prince's doctor to see what he could do. After failing to convince the prince that he was not dead, the doctor reversed his direction and tried to convince his patient that corpses ate just like live people. The crowning touch adopted by the resourceful doctor was to prop a corpse at the dining table to join the prince for dinner. From then until the day he did in fact die the Prince de Condé feasted daily with a corpse that his doctor occasionally replaced with a fresh one when the old one began to look too moth-eaten.

When the distinction between sitting down to dinner and sitting down to a theatrical performance becomes blurred, as in the case of the prince, anything can happen. Usually, though, instead of the ghoulishness that existed around his strange table there is gaiety. A countrywoman of his, Sarah Bernhardt, exemplifies the spirit that usually prevails when dinner becomes spectacle.

For sixty years during the last half of the last century and the first part of this, Sarah Bernhardt was an actress of extraordinary brilliance on both sides of the Atlantic. Hailed as "The Divine Sarah" by an adoring public, wherever she went and whatever she did she never forgot that she was an actress, never stopped performing for her audience. Even as a hostess she remained on stage, playing to her guests. Entertaining in her luxurious Paris home, in her summer retreat, or aboard her private railroad car, she was at one and the same time hostess and actress, playing both roles flawlessly, imaginatively, ceaselessly.

Her dinners in Paris were unique. The mansion was a profusion of massed flowers everywhere, and an orchestra played lively mood music throughout the evening. But the startling feature was The Divine Sarah's menagerie. Romping freely through the rooms would be monkeys, lion and tiger cubs, and perhaps a cheetah or a lynx or an ocelot, while all of the time exotic birds would fly overhead and alight—or perform other, less socially acceptable maneuvers—wherever they saw fit. The Divine Sarah was a compulsive collector of unusual animals and, herself unrestrainably free-spirited, she could not tolerate the idea of confining them in cages.

Lenient and permissive with her animals, Sarah Bernhardt was much less so with her personal staff. Meticulous in her gastronomic standards, she demanded complete perfection from those she employed in her kitchens—and frequently she received it. Sitting at the head of her long, laden table, she was the ringmaster. Sipping champagne—her favorite drink—from an ornate gold goblet presented to her by the lord mayor of London, she stimulated an easy flow of witty conversation around the table, at the same time making sure that the servants were properly attentive to her guests. For their part, the guests felt pampered, well-cared-for by a hostess who lavished her charms on them and by servants who plied them with superb food and vintage wines. Certainly no guest could ever feel ignored—not when a lion or tiger, even if only a cub, contended for a share of his plate. Dinner with The Divine Sarah was an experience not easily forgotten.

The host of one banquet of fairly recent times wished that it had been forgotten but it was not, and because it was not it hastened the arrival of disaster. Stunningly spectacular and awesomely expensive, the banquet was staged by the late Shah Mohammed Reza Pahlavi of Iran in 1971 to mark the 2,500th anniversary of the founding by Cyrus the Great of the Persian Empire from which Iran emerged.

Such pomp, ceremony, and splendor had seldom been seen since the days of Cyrus the Great. To conjure up an atmosphere reminiscent of the Persian Empire that used to be, the Shah erected out in the desert a temporary city of luxurious tented pavilions in which to entertain his five hundred guests from all over the world. To assure himself that the gala feast would be prepared and served with suitable polish and embellishment, he arranged for Maxim's of Paris to fly out to his splendid tent city a battalion of 165 French chefs, wine stewards, and waiters. Among the more fanciful foods prepared by the imported chefs were quail eggs filled with the finest caviar, roast peacock stuffed with *pâté de foie gras,* and saddle of lamb prepared with truffles, the Cadillac among fungi. Throughout the nearly six-hour banquet the guests— planted in thronelike chairs ranging along a mahogany dining table that was a startling 235 feet long—were irrigated by a continuous flow of vintage champagnes, rare wines, and liqueurs to keep them from wilting in the desert heat. The cost for mounting this enormous extravaganza was estimated to be more than $11 million, or more than $22,000 per guest. Such an absurdly excessive and ostentatious squandering of state funds may have been acceptable in Cyrus's day but it was not so in the Shah's. It helped accelerate the rising tide of public discontent that ultimately engulfed the Shah and Iran in tragedy.

The Shah was not the first political figure to discover that when food and spectacle become entwined the outcome can be something that was not anticipated. Nearly a century and a half earlier an American President made the same discovery. Fortunately, this merger of food and spectacle had consequences of much more manageable proportions.

His second term in office was dwindling to just a handful of days and President Andrew Jackson wanted to go out with a flourish. What he was really seeking was a way to render a special thank-you to all the voters who had elected him to office. He decided that he could do it best by giving a reception in the White House to which all citizens would be freely invited. And Jackson knew precisely what food he would serve, at the same time solving a problem that had seemed to be without solution. A dairy cooperative had lately presented him with a gift cheese of mammoth proportions—an edible mountain that tipped the scales at an astonishing 1,400 pounds. He had accepted the gift with expressions of gratitude that were something less than wholehearted because he knew of no way to dispose of so much cheese save for a quiet midnight interment in the White House garden. Now he knew of a way.

On February 22, 1837, the cheese having been maneuvered into position in the state dining room, President Jackson threw open the doors of the White House to the public. They surged in, the masses in a very literal sense. Making the most of this unique opportunity to dine with the President, in a manner of speaking, the visitors elbowed and shoved one another to force their way toward the cheese mountain. By nightfall, when the last of the visitor had finally left, the mansion was a shambles. Gobs of cheese had been ground into the rugs and fragments of it were scattered everywhere, creating a randomly polka-dotted pattern over tables, chairs, and sofas. The walls, especially in the state dining room, were disfigured by the countless imprints left by cheese-stained hands. And permeating the entire mansion was the inescapable odor of the cheese. Ten days later when Martin van Buren succeeded to the Presidency and to the tenancy of the White House the mansion still reeked of cheese.

(Jackson's cheese, huge as it was, would have been dwarfed by a monster produced by Canadian cheese makers as their country's centerpiece at its exhibit in the 1893 Chicago World's Columbian Exposition. It weighed a truly awesome 22,000 pounds. The train carrying it south to Chicago broke down several times under the strain. When it was finally hoisted into position at the Exposition it promptly crashed through the floor of the building.)

If an American President demonstrated that eating can be mass entertainment, an American queen demonstrated that it can also be class entertainment. Mrs. William Astor sat on the throne of American high society during its Gilded Age beginning soon after the Civil War and lasting almost until World War I. She was eminently suited to her queenly role. Her ancestry could be tracked back to Scottish royalty and to Dutch notables and she was married to the multimillionaire grandson of *the* John Jacob Astor. Society's Four Hundred granted her the position of preeminence by reasons of the impeccability of her breeding and the impregnability of her bankbook. (The press had invented the term "Four Hundred" to designate the cream of society because that was the number that could be accommodated comfortably in the ballroom of Mrs. Astor's stately Fifth Avenue mansion.) There was also another reason to yield to Mrs. Astor the dominant role in high society—she knew how to entertain with more finesse and flair than anyone else in town.

The mere act of arriving at Mrs. Astor's for dinner—or for her annual ball, always the third Monday in January—was itself an act of pure theater. Police were on hand to restrain passersby, preventing them from walking in front of the Astor mansion lest they soil the thick-piled, red carpet that had been unrolled over the sidewalk for the arriving guests. As they alighted from their carriages the guests were greeted by applause from the spectators and by bows and helping hands from Mrs. Astor's blue-liveried footmen who escorted them to the door.

Inside one was confronted everywhere by luxury: museum-quality antiques, paintings by the masters, porcelain fireplaces, precious rugs, tremendous Italian candelabra suspended from the intricately carved ceiling of the great hall, a broad marble staircase sweeping to the upper floors, the soft strains of an orchestra, sumptuous arrangements of flowers, an attentive, polished staff of servants. And there, a benign yet commanding presence, was Mrs. Astor, stately in a long gown that served as a rich setting for the magnificent diamonds she always wore. Mr. Astor was usually absent—off sailing on one of his yachts or at his country estate visiting his Thoroughbreds. He was quite content to let his wife rule society alone.

At precisely eight o'clock Mrs. Astor would lead the way into her vast ebony and gold dining room and stand beneath her full-length portrait to greet her guests as they entered. The room would be scented with the perfume of its floral decoration, usually created of four hundred roses, the number chosen of course to symbolize high society's elite Four Hundred. The long table itself would gleam and glitter with the interplay of reflected light from the exquisite crystal and the solid gold plates with which each place was set. Dinner lasted until eleven—the three hours at table would be needed to meet and deal suitably with the twelve gastronomically impressive courses that would be served, together with the half-dozen or so vintage wines the white-gloved stewards would pour.

From time to time various society figures tried to usurp Mrs. Astor's role of preeminence but they could never dislodge her because they lacked her keen awareness of the fine line between luxury and ludicrous ostentation. She would never do as one of her contemporaries did: construct a temporary indoor "pond" and stock it with four swans, who raised a clamor and paddled about furiously as the bemused guests looked on. That wasn't her style.

What was Mrs. Astor's style was the memorable banquet she gave one November evening in 1905 to honor Prince Louis Alexander of Battenberg, nephew of the King of England. All of American society had been pursuing the royal visitor but the sole private invitation he accepted was

Mrs. Astor's. Her other guests that evening were suitably blue-chip, including the daughter of the President. Never had the hostess stage-managed a more flawless or more lustrous banquet. One fact alone suggests the heights she attained that evening—the man she engaged to provide the musical entertainment for her guests was Victor Herbert, conductor of the Pittsburgh Symphony and the nation's foremost composer of operettas.

That banquet for Prince Louis Alexander proved to be Mrs. Astor's last social triumph. A short time later she tumbled and fell on that imposing marble staircase in her mansion. She never recovered from her injuries. Others vied with one another to assume her social position but none could quite make the grade. And then in the aftermath of World War I—when prohibition gave birth to speakeasies and bathtub gin, when Henry Ford put wheels under America, and when hemlines went up and social barriers went down—there was no longer a place for the Gilded Age of society that Mrs. Astor had personified. Dignity gave way to license, radiance lost ground to glossiness, the steak's sizzle became as important as its flavor. Herbert Bayard Swope was to this new kind of social life what Mrs. Astor had been to the old.

Swope did not let inherited wealth deter him from carving out an enormously successful career as a journalist, winning a coveted Pulitzer Prize in 1917 for his war reporting and later winning further acclaim as the hard-hitting editor of the *New York World*. He was at ease in the company of the movers and shakers because he was one of them. He was at ease in the company of the frisky and frolicsome because he was one of them too.

Swope's dinner parties were famous for their good food, for the reliability of the bootleggers who provided the liquid refreshments, for their verve, and for their novel touches. But he outdid himself in 1931 when he gave a banquet in New York to honor the president of the Jockey Club, a group of wealthy horse-fanciers who hired professional jockeys to do their riding for them. The kind of evening Swope arranged required nothing less than the grand ballroom of the swanky Biltmore Hotel. The dinner, though it was a gastronomic achievement of no inconsiderable merit, surprised no one because it was what was expected of both Swope and the Biltmore. It was the spectacular staging of the event that made the evening so unforgettable.

On a signal from Swope the ballroom doors swung open and in trotted twelve Thoroughbreds ridden by jockeys wearing racing silks. The diners roared their enthusiastic appreciation. Then in trotted four more horses, each ridden by a scarlet-coated huntsman equipped with a brass hunting horn. Accompanying these newcomers were eighteen yapping foxhounds. The cheers of the diners, the milling of the horses, and the blaring of the horns turned out to be too much for some of the dogs—they forgot their party manners which only increased the level of the laughter, except among the hotel staff who would have to erase the signs of their transgressions.

Everyone agreed that Bayard Swope's dinner party would never be topped. But then Swope proceeded to top himself. Once more the ballroom doors swung open. This time an artillery caisson, borrowed for the evening from a National Guard regiment, thundered in drawn by four galloping horses.

Among the wildly cheering guests that evening was the governor of New York, Franklin Delano Roosevelt. A few years later, after he had become President, one of his own receptions captured headlines for its unprecedented novelty. The King and Queen of England were in the United States on an official visit and FDR hosted a luncheon in their honor at the Roosevelt estate in Hyde Park, New York. What claimed press attention on both sides of the Atlantic was not the elegance nor the luxury of the occasion—instead, it was its extraordinary informality and unconventionality. Never before had the crowned heads of the British Empire been entertained picnic-style where the main course was hot dogs. Herbert Bayard Swope could appreciate a party like that. Mrs. William Astor would have been appalled.

Chapter Six

RESTORERS OF THE CRYING STOMACH

*Sit down and feed
and welcome to our table.*

WILLIAM SHAKESPEARE

ncreasingly, especially now that society no longer expects female hands always to clutch only a basting spoon and never a briefcase or a slide rule, we are becoming a nation of eater-outers, routinely and habitually dining in restaurants. So it usually comes as a surprise to most of us to discover that the restaurant we take so much for granted is actually a rather modern concept. It was not so terribly long ago that Americans did not agonize over whether they ought to go to a place that specialized in Chinese or Italian or maybe seafood. What they wondered was simply how they would best be able to obtain a meal of any kind outside of the home. It wasn't that nothing at all could be eaten out—it could, but not readily nor conveniently.

The first cooked food ever to become available outside of the home was bread. There were bakeries operating publicly as far back as ancient Rome. Then some enterprising Roman merchants enlarged on the theme by opening stalls along busy thoroughfares to offer passersby cooked meats. Bakeries and meat sellers were later augmented in Europe by shops where one could buy soups. In population centers and along well-traveled highways there were inns where a complete meal could be obtained provided one had rented lodging for the night. In cities and towns there were also "ordinaries" where a single, fixed menu was offered at a single, fixed time. And then there were taverns where limited foods were sometimes available but always only in a minor supporting role to the drink that was the star attraction. (However, America's gift to beef-lovers—the porterhouse steak—originated in a tavern, Martin Morrison's, on the New York waterfront in the early 1800s.)

So one could obtain bed and board or drink and board or a fixed meal that offered no choices or a piece of cooked meat or a bowl of soup, but simply to walk into an establishment to select a full meal from a flexible menu with no strings attached was quite another matter. And then a Frenchman named Boulanger changed all that in 1765 in a landmark development.

Boulanger opened a shop in Paris on the Rue des Poulies where he cooked and served soups to the public. Handy with language as well as with a soup ladle, Boulanger— how appropriate it was for him to be involved with food, since his name translates into English as baker—painted a sign in Latin over the door of his shop. It read: *Venite ad me omnes qui stomacho laboratis et ego restaurabo vos*—"Come to me all whose stomachs cry out and I shall restore you." From the *restaurabo* of his sign comes the word restaurant as a part of dozens of languages from Swedish to Portuguese to Arabic to Russian. But the soup-maker's contribution to language is overshadowed by his contribution to gastronomy.

Boulanger did not want merely to serve soups to the public; he also wanted to offer other foods so that his customers could choose a full meal if they wished. The

trouble was that selling cooked foods was rigidly compartmentalized and controlled in France by official edict as
well as by long-standing tradition. Only the *tripier,* for
instance, was allowed to sell cooked tripe, while only the
traiteur was permitted to sell stewed meats. Although he
was licensed to offer only soups, Boulanger decided to
challenge the system. Boldly one day he cooked a batch of
sheep's feet in a white sauce and offered servings of it to his
customers in addition to his soups. The *traiteur's* guild
immediately brought legal action to halt Boulanger on
grounds that he did not possess a *traiteur's* license to permit
serving stewed meats.

After prolonged deliberation the court rendered its unprecedented ruling. It held that sheep's feet in a white
sauce did not actually constitute a stew and that Boulanger
was therefore not infringing in the domain of the *traiteurs*
and so could not be restrained from offering the dish in his
soup shop. With his historic pot of feet, Boulanger had
broken the iron grip of the monopolies. Boulanger's breakthrough was expanded and exploited to create the complete and flexible menu. The era of the modern, full-
service restaurant was dawning.

If American restaurants in the early nineteenth century
had taken a cue from Boulanger and had posted over their
doors signs beginning with the words "Come to me all
whose stomachs cry out . . ." they would have had to end
lamely with the warning "and leave in the same condition." The truth of the matter is that the American res-

taurant of that period was no place where one could expect to soothe a crying stomach. The food was heavy and greasy, cooked and served indifferently in huge portions as though great quantity could compensate for lamentable quality. (Much of the blame can be pinned on the Mother Country because Britain planted its poor cooking as well as its flag in the New World. Long after the flag had been dislodged from America the handicap of English-style cooking lingered on. Even the English recognize their culinary ineptitude—W. Somerset Maugham, the justly famed British writer, once observed that the only way to cope with England's cooking is to order breakfast three times a day.)

Things began to look up in America in 1831 when two Swiss, John and Peter Delmonico, opened a restaurant in New York. The brothers knew what to do and they knew how to do it. They hired a French master chef to oversee their kitchen and they created menus quite unlike any New York had yet seen. Familiar foods were prepared in new and enticing ways that stimulated the palate. Delectable foods never before encountered in an American restaurant were introduced, among them artichokes, avocados, eggplant, watercress, and truffles. Establishing rigid standards of quality, the Delmonico brothers searched diligently for reliable suppliers who could meet their exceedingly strict requirements. Because many of the fruits and vegetables they sought were completely unavailable in the local markets or could not measure up to their quality standards, the pair bought a large farm in the suburbs to grow their own produce. For the first time New York, and America, had an internationally acclaimed restaurant serving superb food, prepared exquisitely and served gracefully in a sumptuous atmosphere.

The lessons of Delmonico's rubbed off on others, so that gradually other chinks appeared in the wall of despair surrounding America's restaurants. By the mid-1850s Boston had its Parker House, already noted for the Parker House rolls it created and that are still popular today, and for its steaks so tender they could be cut with the side of a fork. New Orleans had its Antoine's with its fabled Creole and French dishes, and San Francisco had its Tadisch Grill where a rich variety of seafood was prepared with the care and skill it deserved. And in New York itself a few restaurants were striving to duplicate Delmonico's level of excellence and some were coming encouragingly close to succeeding. At the Astor House restaurant, for instance, a team of highly trained, specialized chefs was employed exclusively for the wild game on the menu because it offered a choice of almost twenty varieties from canvasback duck, grouse, and wild turkey to venison and terrapin.

As the last half of the nineteenth century got under way one could contemplate without misgivings, and even with pleasure, a visit to many of the restaurants and hotel dining rooms in America's major cities and occasionally even in a few fortunate, smaller ones. But for those who were shuttling around the nation on its expanding network of railroads dining was an ordeal, a test of their ability to absorb punishment. The trains scheduled meal-stops along their routes, but invariably they were at a desolate spot where a crude restaurant existed for the sole purpose of feeding the passengers. All of the advantages rested with these unprepossessing trainside establishments—they dealt with captive audiences who had no other place to go; without competition to keep them straight, their performances were seldom other than utterly deplorable. It was an unwitting act of kindness on the part of the railroads that they never scheduled sufficient time for their meal-stops—at least it compressed passenger misery into a brief time-span.

In 1868 George M. Pullman came to the rescue of the culinarily abused passengers. A few years earlier he had produced the first railroad sleeping cars. Now he designed and produced the first railroad restaurant car; it was placed in service on a run between Chicago and St. Louis.

Pullman's "diner" gave an entirely new dimension of meaning to the word. To start with, it was a model of effective, time-and-step-saving design. (Many of its features would later influence the design of the modern American kitchen.) A gem of efficiency, its compactly engineered work area provided full facilities for complete meal preparation. The car itself—with its carpeted floor, mahogany paneled walls, and crisply starched table linens—looked like a fine restaurant, and its skilled staff treated it like one. Pullman and his diner did for those who traveled what Delmonico's had done for those who stayed put in the city, giving them the prospect of dining well, even luxuriously.

It dawned on railroad management that in their dining cars they had a new marketing tool that could add luster to the company image, so the roads began using the diners competitively to exert gastronomic pressure on one another. Thus, the Baltimore and Ohio became famed for its excellent terrapin stew, the Union Pacific for its antelope steak, and the Denver and Rio Grande for its mountain trout. Any of these specialties, with perhaps oysters on the half shell first and a rich dessert to follow, and a bottle of wine, would cost what would nowadays buy just an ordinary snack. Of course, that was long before prices and dollars had headed in opposite directions, the first toward obesity and the second toward anemia.

The railroad diner generated international admiration, becoming the norm for train travel throughout the civilized world. As in America, diners abroad developed food specialties that became their culinary trademarks. The British railroads, for instance, were noted for their breakfast kippers, smoked to perfection and grilled in creamy butter. A few years ago those kippers erupted into a public controversy that shows the power of food to move one to action.

The distinguished actor, Lord Olivier (at that time Sir Laurence Olivier), had been commuting to London each morning and one of the pleasures of the train trip was the availability of the diner's kippers. However, Lord Olivier was outraged one morning to discover that the railroad administration had unaccountably dropped the kippers from its dining car menu. The actor called a press conference in London to alert the nation to this culinary sabotage, went on TV talk shows to expound on the issue, and in general orchestrated public protest against exile of the kipper from the rails. Recognizing that defeat stared it in the face, management capitulated and announced the restoration of kippers to its menu.

The next morning Lord Olivier was the center of attention when he entered the diner for his breakfast. When he was seated the waiter politely and confidently asked, "Kippers, sir?" Lord Olivier, still smarting from management's actions, gave the knife a gentle twist. "No, thank you," he said blandly, "bacon and eggs."

In this country the railroad diner became so popular that it created a new type of restaurant architecture—the eating place built and equipped to look as though it had just been uncoupled from behind a steam engine. They sprang up everywhere—in cities, in towns, along highways. Unfortunately, these immobile, copycat diners were architectural but not culinary duplicates of the mobile versions. They looked like railroad diners but they didn't taste like them.

This was not the first time that food and architecture had merged. But no alliance of the two was quite so whimsically unusual as that conceived by the Earl of

Dunsmore, a wealthy and delightfully eccentric Scot who loved pineapples, a fruit rarely seen and highly prized in eighteenth-century Scotland. So when a patient Scottish botanist managed to nurse a hothouse pineapple plant into bearing fruit, the first time this had happened so far north, the Earl decided the momentous event needed something equally momentous to mark it. After due consideration of the matter, he assembled architects, sculptors, masons, and artisans and set them to work making a reality of what he conceived to be a fitting salute to Scotland's first pineapple.

When the dust had settled in 1761 and all the workmen had left, what greeted visitors to Dunsmore's estate was a circular stone building in the form of a pineapple, its outer wall painstakingly carved so that it was realistically scored and prickly and its great domed roof terminating in an authentically sculpted crown of stone leaves. The pineapple house measured about 20 feet in diameter and nearly 40 feet from its base to the tip of its spiky crown. Few things gave the Earl of Dunsmore greater pleasure than entertaining his guests in his stone pineapple.

When Dunsmore's pineapple was exactly one hundred years old food and architecture were again linked in a unique way. Though this time the scene was half a world removed from Scotland, nevertheless there was once again a Scottish connection. What was completely different this time was that in 1761 the intention had been to use stone to create the look of food, while in 1861 the intention was to use food to create the look of stone. It happened in Singapore where local authorities assigned a group of Asian convicts to build for the British community a cathedral in honor of St. Andrew, patron saint of Scotland.

Though none of the convicts had actually seen a Western church they agreed among themselves that only marble would be fitting for the exterior of such a building. Undeterred by the unavailability of marble, they devised an ingenious way to make their own from materials at hand. They erected a templelike structure and then set about making "marble" to face it with. First they soaked coconut husks in water to leach their chemicals into the liquid. When the husks had done their job they were removed. Now the convicts added quantities of coarse sugar and egg white to the chemical-laced water, stirring and adjusting the proportions of their ingredients until they achieved the proper consistency. Then they plastered it thickly over the walls of their cathedral. When the plaster dried it was rock-hard and impervious to the elements. But what pleased the convicts most was that after it had been rubbed smooth, their coconut water, egg white, and sugar plaster looked like gleaming, snow-white marble.

The Singapore cathedral and the Dunsmore pineapple would have found favor in the eyes of France's great chef, Marie-Antoine Carême. He, more than any other gastronome, was thoroughly convinced that there was a direct linkage between food and architecture. He insisted, in fact, that the two actually merged into a single entity in the hands of the confectionery chef. Carême always referred to the confectioner's art as "architecture's main branch." Indeed, when he prepared his remarkable table decorations one could never be quite certain whether Carême was a master chef talented in architecture or a master architect talented in cooking.

Carême would begin many weeks in advance to plan the confectionery centerpieces for his special dinners. He would select an architecturally pleasing, historic site as his theme—perhaps a famous palace or a noted temple—then would consult technical references and study engravings of the site to determine its precise dimensions, structural features, and design elements. After all of the specifications were clear to him he would commence slowly and carefully to construct out of spun sugar and pastry dough a confectionery replica that was a faithful, architecturally sound, scaled-down representation of the original. Fellow chefs spoke admiringly of Carême as the architect of French gastronomy, partly because of his voluminous writings interpreting and codifying all aspects of it, and partly because of his brilliant confectionery constructions.

George Pullman, who made such compatible traveling companions out of fine dining and railroading, would have been pleased to dine in the restaurant of the Gare de Lyons, the wondrous railroad station built as one of the jewels of the Paris Exposition of 1900. But even more than Pullman, Carême would have exulted over it because the restaurant had been conceived and executed as an intertwining of superb dining and superb architecture, each adding strength to the other.

Mounting the thickly carpeted, double staircase sweeping up from the station proper to Le Train Bleu, as the restaurant was named, created the impression of approaching a realm that was set quite apart from the ordinary. Even so, one was never really prepared for how much out of the ordinary it actually was. The restaurant's immense rooms looked as though they had been intended to grace a royal palace. The walls and ceilings were virtual art galleries, decorated with magnificent murals, overhead frescoes, intricate carvings, sculpted angels and nymphs. The delicately ornamented crystal chandeliers and wall sconces cast a soft glow over the restaurant's brass fittings, leather upholstered armchairs, white linen cloths, silver serving pieces, and richly brocaded draperies. Along one wall was a bank of tall, arched windows looking out over the station platforms so that one could sit in splendor and tranquility and witness the continuously unfolding scene of trains arriving from far-off places or leaving for them.

This feast for the eye was matched by a feast for the palate. The foods were the finest, the freshest, the most luxurious. Those tracks the restaurant loomed over rushed to its kitchens fruit and vegetables still glistening with the morning dew. Hanging in its aging room to ripen to the exactly right moment for cooking were sides of prize beef and game birds of all kinds. In the holding tank were trout swimming happily in their fool's paradise because they were unaware their holiday would end abruptly the instant the chef had need of them. In the cold storage room were tubs of rich butter and cream, fresh-laid eggs, cheeses from throughout the country. The battery of talented chefs lavished on these premier ingredients all the care and creative skill they deserved. And then the platoon of white-gloved waiters brought the exquisite dishes to table and served them deftly and flawlessly.

Le Train Bleu still graces Paris' Gare de Lyon. And if the restaurant shows its age a bit here and there, if the silver serving pieces and the white gloves are gone and the trout tank is dry, yet it still offers notable architecture and dining intertwined in delightful harmony. Carême, from his place of honor in some heavenly kitchen, surely must look down and beam his approval.

Chapter Seven

BLT, HOLD THE MAYO

*Pray for peace and grace
and spiritual food,
For wisdom and guidance,
for all these are good,
But don't forget the potatoes.*

JOHN TYLER PETTEE

107

n the world of snack foods, America is the undisputed superpower, totally unrivaled for that position by any other nation. (Only those who are mean in spirit and cynical in outlook might ask who would want to compete for such a dubious honor.) It is a position of superiority that sprouted from the humble potato.

The potato seemed destined to remain no more than a simple, staid, humdrum food, the kind that would always be picked out as a blue-collar intruder if it tried to move in white-collar circles. And then American innovation created a whole new dimension to the potato's personality, endowing it with a verve and sparkle it had never before enjoyed. It all took place in 1853 when a domineering industrial tycoon and a thin-skinned redskin crossed paths in Moon's Lake House, a resort in Saratoga Springs, the upstate New York spa favored by the wealthy.

The multimillionaire industrialist was Commodore Cornelius Vanderbilt; the Indian was George Crum, cook in the Lake House kitchen. The Lake House was not the posh sort of place Vanderbilt was accustomed to patronizing; nevertheless, he stopped in one day for lunch. When his food was served he was displeased with the fried potatoes placed before him. Complaining that they had been cut much too thick, he petulantly ordered the waiter to take them back to the kitchen and have them replaced by thinner slices.

Resentful of this criticism of his kitchen performance, Crum set out to teach Vanderbilt a lesson. Snatching up some potatoes, he sliced them to paper thinness, plunged them briefly in boiling oil, sprinkled them liberally with salt, and then sent them out to the table, confident that his critic would get the message. Vanderbilt looked at the unusual slivers of potato, tasted one, smiled, and praised its crispness and flavor. For the balance of the season he returned again and again to Moon's Lake House, bringing his friends along to introduce them to the pleasures of George Crum's "Saratoga chips." Though Crum was denied the satisfaction of getting even with Vanderbilt, at least he lived long enough to see the potato chip he had invented become the cornerstone of a burgeoning snack-food industry.

Today potato chips are established as an international favorite from Tokyo where they are flavored with seaweed, to New Delhi where they are flavored with curry, to Berlin where they are flavored with paprika. In the United States alone manufacturers send about $2 billion worth of potato chips to market each year. A feel for how many chips that amounts to can be gleaned from this awesome statistic: if all those chips were laid end to end they would encircle the globe more than 325 times. By anyone's standards, that's not small potatoes.

By a wide margin the potato chip is the most popular snack food to emerge from America, but it is not the first one to be launched on this side of the Atlantic. What is quite possibly the world's oldest snack, popcorn, is a New World native with a history dating back more than 5,000 years. Popping corn was one of the initial skills the American Colonists picked up from the Indians. It has been said by some, with little apparent basis in actual fact, that as the first Thanksgiving feast was drawing to a close Quadequina, brother of Chief Massasoit, brought out a batch of popped corn to finish off the meal.

Popcorn is overshadowed in importance by the peanut, the snack that comes closest to rivaling potato chips in popularity. Like the others, the peanut is also a native of the Americas. It was cultivated in South America at least 3,800 years ago, was introduced to Africa by Portuguese explorers in the sixteenth century, and then was brought to North America aboard African slave ships.

A St. Louis doctor is credited with creating in 1890 what many consider to be the most exalted state of grace any ambitious nuts can aspire to: peanut butter. Promoting his peanut butter as a readily digestible, tasty, high-protein food, he gained a loyal circle of consumers in the St. Louis area. But it gained national exposure and national popularity when he introduced it at Chicago's Columbian Exposition of 1893. Soon grocers across the country were stocking it in bulk in large wooden tubs to satisfy customer demand. When the innovative agricultural scientist, George Washington Carver, developed an improved version of the butter it attracted even more enthusiasts to the fold. Nowadays it takes about a third of all the peanuts grown in the United States just to satisfy the American appetite for peanut butter. How seriously Americans regard peanut butter becomes quite clear when one notes the presence in Chicago of The American Museum of Peanut Butter History.

Although it is unassailably true that it is in America that the snack enjoys its finest hour, fairness requires recognition that some other countries do make original contributions of their own. But it must be added, again in fairness, that from a distance some of these foreign offerings seem to suggest a form of self-abuse for consumers. A popular Spanish snack is *angulas,* miniature baby eels that look exactly like pale fishing worms and are swallowed whole in a pungent garlic oil. Japanese enjoy snacking on roasted and salted grasshoppers. The French are partial to the pulpy insides of raw sea urchins—spiny, golf ball-sized marine animals. The English are very enthusiastic about baked beans as a snack food. They consume enough baked beans to founder a less stalwart people—nearly 5 million pounds in a single day, much of it in the form of sandwiches.

Viewed against a backdrop of the *angulas,* grasshoppers, sea urchins, and baked bean sandwiches abroad, the American snack scene takes on added savor. Even unrelenting food snobs who profess to see nothing of merit in the American kitchen are forced to concede that when it comes to snacks Americans do seem to have an appealing, innovative touch. What happened to the sausage is proof of that.

There had for a long time been general agreement that the sausage represented one of mankind's happiest, most productive moments in the kitchen. So nearly perfect a food was the sausage that any further improvement was dismissed as unlikely, if not impossible. After all, some sausages were edible without any cooking by the consumer and those that did require cooking called for culinary skill of an irreducibly minimum level, so that even the laziest and most inept could not ruin a sausage. And it came in enough varied flavors, textures, sizes, and shapes so that monotony was not possible even if one ate only sausages, being able to choose among those made of such meats as pork, beef, veal, mutton, goat, chicken, horse, venison, even armadillo, and flavored with such ingredients as beer, wine, milk, eggs, pig blood, tripe, liver, onions, potatoes, rice, oatmeal, herbs, and spices. If all this were not enough to commend it most strongly, the sausage was an overwhelmingly democratic food, comfortably at home with every social class and priced within reach of every economic level.

Considering what a paragon of virtues the sausage is it would seem highly improbable that anyone could perceive in it something that is sinister and disreputable. Yet the improbable came to pass in 1981 when Moroccan police boarded one of their nation's vessels to arrest a French crewmember. The charge against the prisoner? Blaspheming King Hassan II of Morocco. And how had the prisoner committed blasphemy against the king? By removing Hassan's shipboard portrait and in its place hanging a sausage. Surely the delectable sausage deserves a better fate than to be used as a political weapon.

The world's first sausage must have been created fairly soon after Jacob cooked his famous red lentil pottage and traded it off to Esau for his birthright. By the time of the ancient Greeks and Romans, sausages were already widely known. Itinerant Roman hawkers used to sell sausages along the city's busiest streets. One of their best-selling sausages was made of finely diced fresh pork, bacon, nuts, and herbs. These pork sausages were known as *botuli*. In 1735 when European doctors looked for a suitable name with which to label a newly identified disease thought to come from spoiled sausages, they named it "botulism" for the *botuli* of old Rome.

Throughout the thousands of years that sausages have been one of man's favored foods they were adapted and altered and modified according to national tastes but they always managed to remain substantially what they had always been, their changes being changes of degree rather than changes of basic character. Then American culinary imagination came to the fore and fashioned an entirely new identity for the sausage. It emerged as a born-again food.

What American ingenuity did was to take a beef

sausage—the frankfurter that originated in Germany—
and place it within the gently cuddling embrace of a long,
soft bun. Like most great ideas it sounds deceptively
simple but it was a revolutionary development. It en-
hanced the frankfurter with an easy portability and mobility it never before had enjoyed, so that now it was entirely
possible to eat one single-handedly while simultaneously
attending to other matters. Beyond that, the sides of the
bun created a sort of dam rising up along either flank of the
recumbent frankfurter so that mustard and various gastronomic frivolities could be heaped on it with little
danger of overflowing, except when maneuvered by the
hopelessly sloppy.

Some historians credit a vendor at the 1904 St. Louis
World's Fair with being the matchmaker who engineered
the marriage between frankfurter and bun. Others assign
that honor to a hawker in New York's Coney Island in
1867. This version seems to be the more credible since the
frankfurter-in-a-bun was once widely known as a "Coney
Island red hot." Whatever the name it once had, there is no
doubt of the year in which it gained the endearing, enduring, internationally recognized name it now bears. It was
in 1906. T. A. Dorgan, a cartoonist known professionally
as "Tad," was doodling with his pencil as he tried to
brainstorm an idea for a cartoon. What his doodling developed into was a caricature frankfurter, looking like an
elongated dachshund, stretched out in its bun. Tad labeled the houndlike frankfurter in his cartoon a "hot dog"

and the name tickled the public's funny bone so insistently that it gained linguistic respectability and culinary immortality. Today hot dogs are consumed by Americans at the astonishing rate of some 16 billion each year.

Having elevated the hot dog to sausage stardom, American culinary innovators looked around for new heights to scale. They were not long in finding the opportunity they sought.

Back in the mid-1700s France had begun importing beef from Holland by way of the German port of Hamburg. When the beef reached the French restaurants much of it had been chopped and then cooked and served as "Hamburg steak" after the city from which it had arrived. What American kitchen visionaries now did was to take the Hamburg steak, standardize it into a round pattie, give it a hot dog's mobility and convenience by serving it in a bun, and replace its formality with a more easygoing image by streamlining its name to simply "hamburger" with a small "h."

The hamburger became hugely popular. Like the hot dog, it made eating a portable feast and it made eating fun. Once "hand food" had meant chicken, but now there was a growing menu to choose from. What had begun with snacks was now evolving into something else. The evolution gradually shaped that phenomenon of modern life: the franchised world of the fast foods.

Fast-food restaurants are clearly a made-in-America phenomenon. There are the hot dogs and hamburgers and fried chicken. There are the barbecues and the pizzas. (Although the pizza says "Italy" to those who can't see beyond a mere technicality, when it first saw the light of day a thousand years ago it was nothing more than a plain Italian bread; it was only after it became a naturalized American in the mid-1800s that it found its full gustatory potential.) There are the chili, the ribs, the clam rolls, and the sausage biscuits. And there are the colas, especially the colas. John Styth Pemberton may have misfired with his earlier concoctions of Triplex Liver Pills, Indian Queen Hair Dye, and Globe of Flowers Cough Syrup, but the Georgia pharmacist was on target when he compounded a syrup of coca leaves, cola nuts, and other ingredients in a backyard washtub in 1886. Once the claims for its ability to "whiten teeth, cleanse the mouth, harden the gums, and relieve mental and physical exhaustion" were abandoned in favor of promoting it simply as a soft drink, Coca-Cola was a smashing success that, together with the copycat colas, became a mighty river irrigating the fast-food industry.

And then there is the system that America created to make it all work: the streamlining of operation and administration, the mechanization, the central controls, the merchandising, even the distinctive building designs and logos. The system is the real key because it was the element that made possible the creation of great networks of franchised restaurants that were efficiently functional clones of one another, all doing the same things in exactly the same ways just as the advertising jingles promised. There were no surprises and no disappointments because you knew what you were getting into before you ever opened the front door. Thus, every hamburger placed on a McDonald's grill weighed precisely 1.6 ounces and measured 3.875 inches in diameter and .221 inches in thickness, while every one of the Colonel's finger-lickin' good drumsticks was seasoned with the same quantity of the same mix of "secret" herbs and spices. The system bridged geography, language, culture, and politics so that there was a familiar sense of comfortable sameness whether the golden arches cast their neon glow in Melbourne or Montreal or Mexico City, whether the Colonel did his thing in Amsterdam or Altoona.

Although it was created by individual enterprise and initiative, the fast-food world flourishes because it carefully suppresses individualism. Undeviatingly committed to the old adage that too many cooks spoil the broth, the franchisers don't want innovators—or even real cooks—in the outposts of the culinary empires. What they want are obedient employees who will follow instructions from the home office exactly. All of the cooks, the technical staffs, and the planners are back in headquarters with top management studying their computer readouts and experimenting in their test kitchens. Their objective is to refine foolproof formulas for those out in the field and—to the greatest extent possible—to premix, prepackage, and precook the food before it is shipped out from the distribution points.

Critics of the fast-food chains condemn them as neon-lit assembly lines that are to gastronomy what painting-by-the-numbers is to art. They charge that the best things the chains turn out are the catchy jingles in their TV commercials, and they dismiss the food disdainfully as indifferent, dull, and monotonous, served in a plastic, sterile, depersonalized setting. Foreign critics are especially harsh in their appraisal. They get particular satisfaction in heaping abuse on the condiment most associated with fast foods—ketchup, or catsup if you prefer—condemning it as an American food barbarism slowly submerging the planet in a red sea too deep for a Moses to part. Here, at the very least, critics nail the wrong hide to the wall. It was the Chinese who invented the sauce, called *ke-tsiap* in its native land and originally composed mainly of the salted juices of mushrooms and other fungi. It was Dutch and English traders who brought the sauce out of China in the eighteenth century, added tomatoes and otherwise tampered with its formula, and then let it loose on the West. (That other popular fast-food condiment, mustard, is also a native of Asia; the Chinese were using it thousands of years ago.)

Supporters of the fast-food chains praise them as clean, bright, friendly places that invariably deliver a reasonably wholesome, reasonably priced, and reasonably tasty product. What is more, they add, the chains do it speedily, efficiently, and without frittering away time and effort on costly frills that are superfluous, inflating a customer's check without improving his meal.

The truth lies somewhere between the two opposing points of view.

It is clear that if fast foods are not as praiseworthy as their supporters believe, neither are they as blameworthy as their faultfinders charge. Even in the very citadel of gastronomic snobbery and culinary chauvinism— France—fast-food restaurants have made marked inroads. In the Paris area alone there are more than a dozen McDonald's hamburger outlets and that number is targeted to balloon to 166 by the year 2000. So significant a role do fast-food restaurants now play in France that the government, mounting an unwinnable rearguard action to stem the advance of the American chains, has issued an edict banning any official use of the English-language term "fast-food restaurant." But even under its government-mandated label as a *restaurante rapide* serving food that is *prêt-à-manger* (ready to eat) there is no way to hide the fact that it is a wholly American-accented operation. It is also worth noting that the French—who take a perfectly good ham and cheese sandwich and heat it in a special gadget that seals the edges together to frustrate the consumer bent on adding mustard and pickle slices—stand to pick up some worthwhile pointers from America's fast-food expertise.

At the very least, even if one doesn't intend to eat there, a fast-food restaurant is worth a visit just for the show. If things move along as they are supposed to, the staffs put on a carefully choreographed performance that has the grace of a ballet and the economy of movement of a racetrack pit stop.

Chapter Eight

ONE LUMP
OR TWO?

*And a perpetual feast
of nectar'd sweets
Where no crude surfeit reigns.*

JOHN MILTON

here is only one message to be drawn from the fact that three of the most heavily favored words in English for the object of one's affections are Honey, Sweetheart, and Sugar, and that there are similar terms in other languages. The unmistakable message is this: humanity has a universal tendency to confer its love on a couch of carbohydrates, linguistically speaking. This comes as no surprise to anyone who has kept a weather eye on mankind's sweet tooth because humans have lusted after sweets from as far back as anyone is willing to guess.

Honey was man's first, most important sweetening. A carving dating from around 7000 B.C. found on a cave wall near present-day Valencia, Spain, depicts a man gathering honey as bees swarm around him. Ancient paintings discovered in Egyptian tombs show molds used long ago to shape confections that were made of honey mixed with crushed fruits. (If there was one foodstuff the Egyptian could surely count on taking to the tomb with him it was honey—because the substance did double-duty as a food and as a fluid used in embalming the dead.) The Hebrews, Greeks, Romans, and especially the Persians made cakes, confections, and beverages with honey and used it frequently in their cooking. One popular Roman recipe called for cooking ham with honey, and the Bible, in

Exodus 16:31, speaks of manna that was "like wafers made with honey."

One of nature's little ironies is that something as lush and rich as honey should be produced by a tiny creature as austere, inflexible, and relentlessly all-business as honeybees. Realizing what they endure to produce just one pound of honey is enough to move one to sympathy and wonderment. They buzz away from the hive to seek out and alight on flowers that may be many miles distant, sipping from each bloom nectar that they deposit in their special honey stomachs. When the bees have all the nectar they can handle at one time they head back to the hive; while in flight enzymes they secrete in their stomachs are working on the nectar to convert it into a sugary liquid. When the bees reach the hive they regurgitate the liquid and immediately fly back to the flowers for more nectar. Meanwhile, within the hive other bees work the liquid ceaselessly to evaporate excess moisture and make it thick and viscous. And in the end, after some 25,000 flights to about 2.5 million flowers and after all the sipping, converting, regurgitating, and working has produced its pound of honey, along comes a human to carry it away and ship it off to ennoble the hot cakes of someone who neither knows nor cares what the bees endured to create such gastronomic pleasure.

Life was not so heartless for the bees of India where they were less likely to see their hard-earned honey winding up on someone else's plate. It was not that Indians did not have as big a sweet tooth as others elsewhere, it was that they were not so dependent upon honey to satisfy it because they had an alternative that existed nowhere else in the world—a plant that yielded a sweetening. At least 5,000 years ago Indians were extracting sweet crystals from this native, reedlike grass. Gradually over the centuries, knowledge of this wonderful plant began to creep eastward toward Indochina and westward toward Arabia. In the fourth century B.C. one of Alexander the Great's generals wrote in amazement of the Indian "honey-bearing reed that produced its bounty without the aid of bees." When farmers in Arabia began cultivating the Indian plant they adapted its name from *sarkara* in the Sanskrit of ancient India to *sukkar* in Arabic.

In the eighth century the Moors swept northward from Arabia into Europe where they subjugated Spain. They brought with them much that was new to the Spanish, including three strange foods: spinach, rice, and *sukkar*. The Spanish were not quite convinced that spinach was such a good idea but they doted on the rice and the *sukkar*, planting the latter along the south coast where the climate was favorable to it and altering its name to *azucar*. Not until the eleventh century, when Crusaders returning from their wars in the Middle East brought it with them, did the sweetener reach the rest of Europe, and even then it was only in extremely limited amounts. Sugar, as it was called in English, was in such short supply in Europe that it was priced out of reach of all except the wealthy. The poor continued to rely on honey or they went without.

It was Christopher Columbus who made it possible for the poor to reach into the sugar bowl. On his second voyage to the New World in 1493, he brought sugarcane to Santo Domingo where it flourished in the hospitable soil and sun. After that initial success, sugar plantations began springing up throughout the West Indies and in Brazil on the mainland. Fifty years after Columbus introduced the plant to the New World, in London alone two refineries were kept busy processing the cane arriving from the Americas.

What started with Columbus was completed in 1878 at the Paris World's Fair where the first practical and inexpensive process for the large-scale extraction of sugar from beets was demonstrated. Now the cold-weather countries could grow beets to produce their own sugar just as the hot-weather countries had been doing with their cane. Sugar, whether from beets or from cane, was now a truly universal, abundant, and cheap sweetener.

With sugar so easily available, the world could now give free rein to its sweet tooth, especially in taking advantage of a food from the Americas. In the early 1500s Spanish explorers reaching Central America had been introduced to *cacahuatl,* a bitter Aztec drink made mainly from the pounded beans of the cacao tree. The bitterness of the beverage put the Spaniards off but they discovered that by adding sugar to the liquid they could transform it into a very pleasant drink. To distinguish the Spanish version from the unsweetened *cacahuatl* the Aztecs named it *chocolatl*.

For the next hundred years chocolate was a favored drink among the upper classes in Spain. Wanting to keep a good thing to themselves, they kept it secret from the rest of Europe for a long time but then, like all secrets do eventually, it leaked out. In 1615 chocolate drinking made its appearance in French royal circles. Then Spanish monks seeking converts in Germany brought that country chocolate as well as the Church. In 1657 a shop in London advertised that it had for sale to the public "an excellent West Indian drink called chocolate." By the end of the century there were chocolate shops serving the drink almost everywhere in Europe. But in the North American colonies, closer to the source of the cacao bean, the first chocolate was not drunk until 1755.

The high regard in which chocolate had come to be held is readily apparent in the scientific name assigned to cacao in 1720 by the Swedish botanist, Carolus Linnaeus, during his monumental classification of the world's plant life: *Theobroma cacao,* Greek for "cacao, food of the gods." (Both the tree and its beans are called cacao; the powder manufactured from roasted cacao beans after a portion of their butterfat has been removed is called cocoa.)

But the "food of the gods" was not without its share of controversy. There were some who claimed that chocolate was a threat to health, that it induced fevers and poisoned the system. Others argued just the opposite, insisting that it restored strength and prolonged life. Some attacked chocolate on moral grounds, claiming that it had an aphrodisiac effect on those who drank it, while others—hoping for the best—sought it out precisely for that alleged quality. To sell the public chocolate and yet not become embroiled in the dispute that swirled around it, two Parisians hit upon a clever stratagem: they opened a pharmacy and dispensed chocolate on demand as a medical potion. By draping the mantle of medicine around chocolate they sidestepped the tug-of-war over it as a foodstuff. The shop, Debauve et Gallais, is still going strong in Paris, long ago abandoning its role as a pharmacy to emerge as a premier *chocolatier* with few equals anywhere.

During the eighteenth century, as a result of English, Dutch, and especially Swiss developments, methods were devised to make chocolate do more things in more ways. Techniques were devised to convert it into a solid that could be eaten, to make it readily and smoothly meltable at mouth temperature, to enrich it with milk and with flavorings, and to form it into a powder for baking and cooking uses. The day of the chocoholic was dawning— and if one had to become addicted to something, surely there were many worse choices than chocolate.

In the meantime in the early seventeenth century, while chocolate was slowly making its transition from a bitter Aztec drink to a sensual gastronomic temptress, a French chef had been exercising his creative talents in a way that would bring fresh joy to sweets-lovers everywhere. What the chef was seeking to do was to induce young Prince Charles Phillipe de Condé, the king's grandnephew, to eat a balanced diet instead of only the sweet things the boy insisted upon. The solution the resourceful chef settled on was to take the foods the child obstinately rejected and to disguise them within a concealing and enticing glaze of sugar, egg whites, and nuts. With eyes only for the sweet coating the boy was in this way lured into eating the nourishing fillings along with the tasty glazings. Dishes prepared in this manner came to be called "candied" after young de Condé for whom they had been created. When the public later developed a great fondness for the glazing, simply for its own sake, it became "candy." This was the first of two notable encounters the Prince de Condé would have with food. The second one, described in an earlier chapter, occurred after he had become old and senile.

After candy made its appearance, and after eating-chocolate later came along to join it, it was inevitable that some inspired culinary matchmaker would think to arrange a wedding of the two. Now, with chocolate and candy available either coupled or separately, the public's ever-hungry sweet tooth was coddled and gratified (as well as riddled with cavities) as never before. On every side came an accelerating outpouring of new varieties, new flavors, and new combinations. There were sweets to be chewed, licked, crunched, or simply allowed to melt in the mouth, confections that were filled with creams, nuts, caramels, jellies, fruits, liqueurs, or nougats, candies that were shaped like bars, cubes, circles, balls, or rolls. Imaginations soared on saccharine clouds and never returned to earth.

The Germans proudly produced a chocolate soup and the Irish a chocolate sandwich. The Italian province of Parma, already famed among gourmets for the Parmesan cheese it invented, gained fresh gastronomic luster by creating candied violets. The Danes coated boiled potatoes with caramel, while over in Canada's smallest province the Prince Edward Islanders made a fudge of mashed potatoes, coconut, sugar, and chocolate. When he was the occupant of the White House, President John F. Kennedy brought fresh warmth to Anglo-American relations by letting it be known that he was devoted to English toffee, and when Ronald Reagan made it into the White House he elevated the jelly bean to a status symbol. Across the Potomac, one of the most intriguing bits of information to filter out of the Pentagon's subbasement, supersecret war room is that the Joint Chiefs of Staff keep a dish of hard candies on their conference table to help them in their deliberations. But the British refuse to yield to anyone in their adoration of sweets. Consuming candy at a greater clip than any other people in the world, they do away with more than 25 pounds per person per year. It leads one to believe that the stiff upper lip for which the British are so much admired may not result from steadfastness as much as from pressure of the dental work under it to repair the ravages of all that candy.

One would suppose that the world's enduring and impassioned love affair with candy would leave everyone too exhausted to muster quite the same level of enthusiasm for any other way to satisfy the insistent craving for sweets. Not so. Mankind has managed to carry on with equal ardor and energy a simultaneous romance with that velvety smooth, cooly seductive enchantress: ice cream.

Who it was that had the initial spark of genius that led to creation of ice cream is uncertain; what is not uncertain is that there are many claimants for that honor. Italians are always pleased to point out that the ancient Romans, those who could afford the luxury, dispatched fleet-footed runners to the mountains to bring down snow for a cooling, flavored dessert. Nero, for one, was partial to it; his recipe called for honey, fruit pulp, and wine to be mixed with the snow. Of course, that was not really ice cream but was instead a form of sherbert; if Nero had frozen it around a stick he would have wound up with a popsicle. Anyway, the Aztecs and the Persians also made snow desserts. The Persians, in fact, called theirs *sharbah,* from which the term sherbert comes.

In the thirteenth century Marco Polo returned to his native Venice from his seventeen-year sojourn in China, India, and other parts of the East. Included in his long account of all the strange things he had encountered in his travels was a description of an icy dessert that included milk among its ingredients. Although it was still a kind of sherbert, it was at least getting within hailing distance of ice cream. During the next two or three centuries all Europe was busy making sherberts, sometimes with milk.

It was during the sixteenth century that actual ice cream made its appearance, some say first in France, others say first in Italy. Even if it were possible to pin down the truth it would only indicate the technical birthplace of ice cream. To find out where, in a larger and less technical sense, it was *really* born one must look farther westward. Only those who are unimaginative and petty would deny that the real home of ice cream, the place where it was cherished and refined and guided to greatness, was America.

From the very moment of the birth of this nation, Americans regarded ice cream in a special way. When he was inaugurated first President of the United States in 1789, George Washington noted in the inventory of his possessions that he was the owner of "two pewter ice cream pots." The next summer, with the national capital temporarily in New York, Washington ran up a bill there for ice cream to the tune of $200, a great sum for the time. Thomas Jefferson, the third President, was as much an ice cream freak as the first, serving it frequently at the White House. Jefferson was a man who took his food seriously, importing a French chef to take charge of the White House kitchen and then assigning two out of the mansion's staff of eleven to serve as his apprentices. Very often the President puttered about the kitchen himself. During one of his more fruitful putterings he invented a luscious dessert: ice cream surrounded by a quickly browned pastry coating. It would later become known as baked Alaska everywhere except in France. The French, apparently reluctant to concede that an American could devise such a gastronomic blue blood, persist in calling their version of a baked Alaska a Norwegian omelette, which does seem to puzzle Norwegians.

Like Jefferson, Nancy Johnson had a weakness for ice cream and used an agile imagination to do something about it. What she did, in 1846, was to render a signal service to mankind by inventing the hand-cranked ice cream freezer. With her innovative breakthrough she brought to every home the capability of easily and readily becoming its own ice cream parlor. Unfortunately, Nancy Johnson was infinitely more accomplished as an inventor than as a business executive. She forgot to obtain a patent for her marvelous machine and so had to be content with personal satisfaction while William G. Young, shrewdly obtaining a patent for the Johnson freezer, reaped all the material rewards.

In 1867 at the Paris Universal Exposition the United States pavilion had a gastronomic hit on its hands—the only bright spot of the entire American display—when it introduced to Europe a new American confection that was both food and drink: the ice cream soda. It presented opportunities for experimenting with flavor combinations that gave promise of a saccharine whole that was greater than the sum of its parts. But even this was surpassed in the early 1890s by the invention of the sundae, some say by Ed Berner in Two Rivers, Wisconsin, while others give the nod to an anonymous confectioner in Evanston, Illinois. What is important is not the identity of the creator but the character of the creation. What it did was to open up a whole new, high-calorie world of opportunity for ice cream-lovers. Now wherever their flights of fancy might beckon them—to syrups, fudge, whipped cream, nuts, butterscotch, marshmallow, no matter the whim—they were free to go, taking a spoonful of this and a portion of that to mound on a welcoming bed of ice cream. Mankind could now sink its sweet tooth into an embarrassment of riches.

But America was not yet content to rest on its laurels. In 1904 came the cone, introduced at the St. Louis Exposition as an edible depository for a scoop of ice cream. It was an instant success because it did for the cream what the bun had done for the hot dog and the hamburger; it endowed it with an easy mobility that made it a portable pleasure. Portability assumed fresh dimensions in the early 1920s with invention of the Eskimo Pie, the Good Humor, and the Dixie Cup, all in rapid succession. Then came the great wave of innovation that began in the 1930s and still surges onward: the explosion of new flavors and exotic combinations. This began the golden age of ice cream. Never before had tastebuds been so tantalized, palates caressed so seductively. And never before had language sparkled more engagingly. This was the time when mankind was presented with such sterling gifts as heavenly hash, rocky road, rum raisin, mocha chip, and banana mango. (It may help ease the pangs of guilt for the calorie-conscious to know that a normal serving of that traditional American dessert, apple pie, usually contains twice the number of calories of two scoops of vanilla ice cream.)

The quest goes on, the striving to produce even richer, more voluptuous, more creamy ice creams. And the public responds happily in the only way that is meaningful and appropriate—with spoons upraised and tongues at the ready. The statistics tell the tale. Ice cream consumption in the United States now stands at about 800 million gallons annually, which places an ocean of jamoca-almond-fudge between Americans and the next most avid consumers of ice cream, Australians. Among Americans it is—somewhat strangely, considering their climate—the Alaskans who wield the biggest cone; they eat ice cream at a rate that is twice greater than the national average.

Those who take comfort from such things can debate endlessly the question of whether it was the Italians or the French who invented ice cream. But among the fair-minded there can be no debate over who has conquered it, who has nurtured and guided and molded it into a state of sublime gastronomic eminence. Why else would the residents of Kuwait, Panama, Singapore, and scores of other discerning and fortunate places around the world joyfully flock to local emporiums to be granted the sweet benediction of American ice cream?

With the craving for sweets rooted so deeply and spread so widely, who has the biggest sweet tooth of all? Is it the British with their cakes and tarts and trifles, their jams and jellies and marmalades, and their record consumption of candies of all kinds? Is it the Americans with their pies and Twinkies and Fig Newtons, their Milky Ways and Tootsie Rolls and Hershey bars, and their record consumption of ice cream and soft drinks? No, it is neither. The sweetest tooth of all, if it hasn't already rotted out, is in a Bulgarian mouth. The latest available statistics reveal that the Bulgarians consume more sugar than anyone else in the world, on the order of 140 pounds per person per year. Now *that's* a sweet tooth.

Chapter Nine

EMILY POST, WHERE WERE YOU WHEN WE NEEDED YOU?

*Tell me what you eat,
and I will tell you what you are.*

ANTHELME BRILLAT-SAVARIN

rillat-Savarin was stretching the truth for the sake of coining an attention-getting aphorism. He would have been on much firmer ground had he instead said, "Tell me *how* you eat and I'll tell you *who* you are." There is a simple test that will make believers of skeptics who consider that this version makes no closer approach to reality than does Brillat-Savarin's original assertion. All that is required is a plate of soup.

Consider this: if you begin your dinner with the soup you are a Westerner, but if you end your dinner with the soup you are Japanese. On the other hand if you eat your soup for breakfast you are probably Cambodian, possibly Chinese. If you eat your soup and everything else at the meal with your right hand only, never using your left, you are a devout Moslem. If while you are eating your soup you tilt your plate away from you, you are an American who is watching his table etiquette. However, if you tilt your plate toward you, you are either a European or the kind of American who might feel a bit ill at ease with a finger bowl.

The soup plate is merely one among a large cast of mealtime tattletales. The plain truth is that a peek into the dining room, more than merely revealing whether or not leftovers are on the schedule again, will speak volubly to anyone who knows how to listen. A single, quick glance at the table at breakfast time in medieval Ireland would reveal clearly the social status of those who would be coming to that table. If there was a cup of water to mix into the breakfast oatmeal it was a workman's table. If instead of the water there was milk it was a chieftain's table. And if there was honey in addition to the milk it was a royal table.

Even so simple a matter as the way the seating is arranged around the table can be revealing. In the Athens of 2,500 years ago one did not simply sit down to a meal, one also sat down to a demonstration of male chauvinism in action. The women and children took their meals together at small tables. Those supposedly superior creatures, the men, dined at separate tables attended by solicitous servants. Even more marked was the difference in the way that the diners were placed at their tables. The women and children were seated on simple chairs, whereas the men reclined in pairs on double-wide couches.

In Japan the question of whether one ought to seat a dinner guest on a chair or stretch him out on a couch never had a chance to come up. No seating at all was provided. All of the diners knelt on floor mats and leaned back on their heels. The women were required by strict custom to eat unobtrusively in total silence. Japanese men, on the other hand, were expected to indicate their pleasure over the meal by belching politely from time to time. Not to belch as one ate was to lose face by revealing one's lack of good breeding.

Interestingly, although chauvinism was quite readily

apparent in the dining customs of many lands from Athens to Japan, and even though chauvinism is a term that the French coined, it did not intrude itself between the sexes at the dinner tables of the medieval French. This may perhaps have been because the typical homes of even the well-to-do were so sparsely furnished, so uncomfortable, and so drafty that everyone was too busy in winter trying to keep warm and was too overcome in summer by the odor of the dogs and cats allowed to swarm around the table to give thought to the battle of the sexes.

In France the men and women were paired off at meals, seated either on stools or on benchlike *bancs* (from which the word "banquet" would later evolve). The diners usually shared one cup per couple and served themselves with their hands. First-time visitors were invariably surprised when the desserts were brought to the table—almost always they included pastries shaped by freewheeling, ribald bakers to resemble male and female genitals. The medieval French bakers were, at least in spirit, the advance guard of the platoon of dirty postcard hawkers that would swarm around later generations of foreign visitors.

Across the Channel in England meals were also lively, uninhibited, and crude affairs but the tone here was not set by bawdily imaginative bakers as in France. Here the levity and the animation were fueled by the "black jacks," the tremendous, leather tankards of beer that were central and popular features of the table. All of the English, whether high-born or commoner, were passionately fond of their beer, a habit that still lingers on. Queen Elizabeth herself usually breakfasted—even as a young child—on beer, salted herring, and brown bread, and nobody in medieval England thought it at all strange. The beer and herring combination pleased her because the saltiness of the fish induced a greater thirst for the beer. One gallon of beer per person was considered a usual and conservative daily allowance for everyone, including nuns in convents. By the time the main meal of the day was served the effects of the breakfast beer were still being felt because the normal dinner hour in Europe during the Middle Ages was around ten in the morning. Supper was a light meal taken in the late afternoon. Centuries would pass before dinner would become an evening meal.

Throughout Europe of that era meals were boisterous and table manners were crude. Even the table itself was crude, often only loose boards laid across a pair of trestles resembling today's sawhorses. (Reminders of those table boards can be found in the expression "bed and board.") It was the general custom in winter to go to table bundled in hats and outer garments in an effort to ward off the chill that seeped into the homes of the rich as well as the poor, since the homes of neither were weathertight. Awkwardly bundled up as they were, the diners were certain to wind up with random patterns of food stains over their clothes. Furthermore, napkins had not yet come into vogue, so greasy fingers were wiped dry on one's clothing or on the tablecloths that had begun to appear in some parts of

Europe in the thirteenth century. To make matters worse, or at least messier, it was considered great sport by many to enliven mealtimes by throwing bits of food at one another. One account describes how a female diner at the French royal palace during the reign of Louis XIV joyfully poured a bowl of salad over the King's daughter. If it is true that cleanliness is next to godliness, then the medieval dining table must have been a remarkably ungodly place.

It is, of course, quite unfair to judge the past from the perspective of the present, to measure it by modern yardsticks. The fact is that sometimes it was at least partly a case of doing the best one could with what one had available. In ancient Athens the only eating implement routinely available at the table was a spoon. All solid foods were necessarily eaten with the fingers because the only alternative was to go unfed. The Athenian did make an attempt to keep those fingers clean and dry by blotting them with scraps of bread from time to time during the course of the meal. (However, when a Roman was invited to dinner he had the foresight to bring with him a *mappa*, a linen on which to wipe his hands and mouth.)

Even centuries after the Athenians a spoon was still the only individual eating implement one could count on finding on the European table. If it was necessary for a diner to reduce his portion of solid foods to more manage-able size it was a case of tear it apart by hand or cut it with the personal knife that was carried routinely by almost everybody.

If utensils to eat with were scarce in medieval Europe, utensils to eat from were equally as scarce. Wooden, earthenware, pewter, and even silver platters and bowls— the type depending upon one's social and economic standing—were available to bring the food to the table. However, once that food reached the tables there were no individual plates to eat it from, except in the homes of the very wealthiest and even there they were often scarce. Even soups were routinely drunk from a communal bowl, although in more pretentious households there were frequently four soup bowls, one on each corner of the table, to save diners having to reach so far.

In France well into the thirteenth century and even into the early fourteenth century, when guests sat down to a meal they expected the servants to bring each of them a *tranchoir,* a large, round, flat slab of hard-baked bread. This became the diner's individual plate as he piled on it the foods he selected from the serving platters. By the time the meal had come to an end the *tranchoir* had become saturated with the juices of all the foods that had been heaped on it. If the diners were in a generous mood they would leave the *tranchoirs* for the servants to eat as a reward for having been attentive to their needs. However, the guests often polished off their *tranchoirs* themselves; for that reason a hearty eater came to be called a trencherman.

The first to make a break with the coarseness and crudeness that were so characteristic of mealtimes in medieval Europe were the Italians. They were at that time almost the only custodians of whatever sensitivity and finesse were to be found in Europe. It was they whose innovations would mold and shape dining customs and manners into the form that is in general use today throughout the West.

It was early in the twelfth century that the fork made its initial appearance in Italy. It was a small, two-tined affair introduced by the wife of the Doge Domenice Silvie, the chief magistrate of Venice. A lady of some delicacy, she had simply grown tired of the messiness of eating everything with only the fingers. The fork of the Dogaressa of Venice was for a long time a novelty copied by only a handful of noble Venetian families. Some decades would pass before the custom spread to a number of important households in other major Italian centers. Then the conviction began to grow that the fork was not a silly, frilly affectation but was actually an extremely practical, efficient tool and its adoption moved along more rapidly. By the 1500s it had become common practice throughout Italy for tables to be set with individual knives, forks, and spoons. Usually they were made of brass, although in the more affluent homes they were frequently of silver.

The rest of the Italian table setting had progressed in tandem with its eating implements. Graceful, exquisitely decorated Venetian glassware was now more and more in evidence, as were ornate platters and serving pieces beautifully crafted of silver. Quite popular were individual plates and bowls made of majolica—an attractive earthenware that was enameled and glazed. Everything was laid out on fine table linens that had been embroidered intricately. And even the table itself had undergone a transformation. It was no longer merely crudely utilitarian; now it had become a handsomely crafted, lavishly carved piece of furniture.

The grace and the elegance—to say nothing of the vastly improved level of sanitation—that Italy had introduced into the dining room did not turn out to be easily exportable conditions. They were glacially slow in finding wide and willing acceptance beyond Italy's borders. A sixteenth-century German preacher, learning of the fork that the Italians had adopted, warned his countrymen not to follow suit because to do so would be to oppose God's very clear intention that men should eat with the hands that He had provided them. Farther to the west in that same period, Englishmen and Frenchmen were being told that good manners required that they wipe their noses with their "knife hands"—handkerchiefs having not yet come on the scene—rather than with their "eating hands" lest they run the risk of upsetting any who had to reach into the platters of food after them.

By the end of the century the Italian style of eating had taken root throughout most of Europe, first among the aristocracy and the wealthy and then—at a more deliberate pace—among the rest of the population. By the mid-1600s the Dogaressa's fork was in virtually everyone's hand, even the Germans who apparently had not become convinced that their Creator would disapprove. America already had its first fork. John Winthrop had brought it with him in 1630 when he had set sail from England aboard the *Arbella* to take up his post as the first governor of the Massachusetts Colony. For a long time his was the only fork known to be in use in the New World.

One of man's failings, among the many that are a part of the human condition, is that he seldom knows when to call it quits. As a result, as society retreated farther and farther from the crudeness and coarseness of medieval Europe, it simply kept going until it found itself approaching closer and closer to excesses in the opposite direction. The fork makes a good mirror to reflect the way society worked itself from one extreme to the other because the fork constitutes a prime example of what took place.

It took nearly five centuries from the time the Dogaressa of Venice picked up her first two-tined fork until it became routinely accepted throughout the West. But once Westerners finally learned to hold a fork in their hands they went overboard. As the sixteenth century gave way to the seventeenth, and then to the eighteenth and nineteenth, the fork multiplied into a vast, bewildering family of forks accompanied by strict rules of table etiquette to govern the socially proper usage for each different kind of fork. There was one fork for eating meats and a different one for eating fish. There was a special fork for salads, one for fruit, and still another for desserts. There were special forks for eating shrimp, for eating snails, and for eating cheese fondues. There were forks of one size for use at dinner and forks of a different size for use at lunch. There were special forks for serving meats and others for serving cheese, forks for pickles, and still others for lemons.

This unrestrained creation of forks of all kinds was accompanied by a similar multiplication of special-purpose spoons, knives, plates, and glasses so that a table set for an elaborate banquet had become a complicated challenge. But even all of this did not take the steam out of society's zeal to replace the earlier excesses of the medieval dining room with excesses of its own invention. It turned its attention next to the bawdiness that had been the most consistent flavor of those earlier meals, searching for opportunities to transform delicacy into a detergent to wash away all signs of that ribald past.

As usual, society found a way to go too far. Scrutinizing anatomy through the eyes of an overzealous prude, society insisted on reconstructing the bodies of the animals that found their way into the cookpot. A chicken no longer had a breast or a thigh; instead, it now had white meat and a second joint. The cow, too, was denied its breast and in its place was given a brisket. The lamb, by a similar bit of dinner-table linguistic surgery, had its testicles replaced by fries. Eventually society came to its senses and abandoned many of its contrived, artificial terms but some had already become too firmly fixed to be shaken loose.

Modern America seems to have mastered one way to steer a middle course between the excesses that have so often hovered over the dining table. America does it with a backyard, a barbecue grill, and a good sauce for the ribs. A large segment of the world, as much as half of the total population by some estimates, has its own method of avoiding the entanglements of the dining room. It eats with its fingers while squatting on the ground near the cookfire—just as it was in the beginning.

Chapter Ten

THE LAST WORD

*Food is a subject of conversation
more spiritually refreshing
even than the weather, for the number
of possible remarks about
the weather is limited, whereas of food
you can talk on and on and on.*

A. A. MILNE

ilne could have gone even further in pointing out the difference between food and weather as subjects of conversation. He could have added that everybody talks about the weather but nobody does anything about it, whereas everybody talks about food and everybody—or so it often seems—does something about it in his own individual way. Food has the power to arouse, to stimulate, to inspire, to move people to action. For every foodstuff, no matter how minor its role, there is someone out there waiting to shower affection on it and to become an active partisan in its behalf.

Take, as an example, the anchovy. A food fish so small and so insignificant as the anchovy could be assumed to easily escape anybody's serious attention. Yet the poet Sidney Smith found himself completely captivated by the anchovy. Glimpsing in the tiny fish qualities that had escaped more casual observers, he paid homage to it in the manner that he knew best: he wrote an ode to the anchovy. In his poem he revealed that the secret of elevating a salad to a position of gastronomic superiority is to add a spoonful of chopped anchovy to its dressing. Not to be outshone by Smith's iambic pentameter salute to the anchovy, a professional colleague, Pablo Neruda—eminent Chilean man of letters and winner of the Nobel Prize in Literature—wrote a poem about hot peppers.

Like Sidney Smith, Gioacchino Antonio Rossini, composer of such popular operas as *The Barber of Seville,* was an admirer of the anchovy. He also was partial to a few other dainties and he honored them ensemble by composing a quartet of piano pieces entitled, "Radishes, Anchovies, Pickles, and Butter Themes and Variations." Gastronomy returned the compliment when a prominent chef devised a new filet of beef dish and christened it *tournedos* Rossini in recognition of the musician's devotion to food. (Giacomo Meyerbeer, another prominent operatic composer, received even more gastronomic salutes than his friend, Rossini. When Meyerbeer's opera, *L'Africaine,* was unveiled in 1865 it was a smashing success that moved chefs to create more than a dozen new dishes, all of which they called *L'Africaine* in tribute to Meyerbeer.)

If the anchovy has been effective in stimulating the flow of artistic juices among its admirers, it has been outclassed in that respect by other small denizens of the sea: shellfish. Oliver Wendell Holmes paid poetic homage to shellfish when he penned his famous "The Chambered Nautilus." More often, however, artists reached for chisels and knives instead of pens when they set about the task of giving shellfish their artistic due. Museums from China to Holland exhibit carvings and sculptures of all types that use the scallop shell as their central design theme. Even as far back as ancient Pompeii the scallop had already become a great favorite as a design motif for the decoration of homes and of artifacts.

Henri Toulouse-Lautrec, the brilliant French painter who was endowed with giant creative talent as though to compensate for the deformed legs that dwarfed him, insistently contended that gastronomy was as much a genuine art as painting. His words could not be dismissed lightly because he was so notably competent to speak for both pursuits. As skilled with his basting spoons as with his paintbrushes, he happily bustled about his kitchen devising new dishes or preparing cherished old ones. It seemed not to bother him that as he moved about his feet tangled in the apron that forever trailed the ground no matter how much he hoisted it up. Hanging proudly in the Museum of Albi is a portrait of the aproned artist busily baking at his oven.

With Toulouse-Lautrec it was sometimes difficult to determine whether it was the palate or the palette that was his chief passion. Often he found the time to combine them both in a way that amused and pleased him: painting exuberant covers for the menus of restaurants whose kitchen performance he considered to be praiseworthy. Once he and a friend booked passage on a small freighter for a painting holiday in North Africa. When Toulouse-Lautrec came aboard he brought with him hampers of lobster and fresh-caught fish. Then he set up an impromptu, temporary kitchen in the boiler room where he cooked away quite happily throughout the voyage.

Toulouse-Lautrec was only one in a long procession of artists who found that food and painting could have a strong affinity for one another. The very first paintings that man created, those that some primitive ancestors fashioned on cave walls in Spain and France, portrayed the animals that were hunted for food. Later artists continued to depict food animals but now they broadened their interests to also portray foods that had mythological or religious symbolism.

It was left to a Venetian, Jacopo de' Barbari, to become the first ever to paint food simply because it was artistically worthy of being painted for its own sake. In 1504, de' Barbari arranged a fresh-killed partridge and other foodstuffs into a grouping that was pleasing to his artist's eye. Then he proceeded to paint the grouping he had arranged, thus creating the world's first still life. That initial still life had a marked effect on artists. It stimulated them to look at foods differently, to perceive in them forms, textures, and colors that made them as appropriate to the studio as they all along had been to the kitchen. Still lifes became a firmly established part of the world of art. Throughout the sixteenth and seventeenth centuries the Dutch, especially, produced brilliant paintings of fish, game, fruits, and vegetables arranged in kitchen and dining-room settings. In the following century the French came into their own as painters of food scenes. Given the Frenchman's deep attachment to food it was inevitable.

The first American still life, a painting of fruit, was executed by Charles Willson Peale just before the Revolutionary War. However, to think of Peale only as an artist is to miss out on the surprising, colorful dimensions of the man. He started out as a saddlemaker in his native Maryland, soon left for London to study art, returned to America and established a studio in Philadelphia, commanded a company of soldiers during the Revolution, and invented a number of devices, including new types of bicycles, eyeglasses, and false teeth. In whatever spare time he had he pursued two hobbies: taxidermy and archaeology. It was as an amateur archaeologist that he unearthed—in 1801 in Newburgh, New York—the first complete mastodon skeleton.

However, it is as an artist that Peale is best remembered. A prolific painter, he completed a great number of canvases, among them many still lifes, but those that claimed the most attention were the portraits he did of George Washington. The Father of the Country posed for Peale more often than for any other artist. Nobody is certain of the number of portraits that resulted from all those sittings but the estimates run as high as sixty. One critic of the period sniffed disapprovingly at the Peale portraits, claiming he made Washington seem to be "pig-eyed."

Peale could always be counted on to do things on a grand scale, so when he began to raise a family he did not call it quits until he had fathered seventeen children. Of his children, five were boys and he named each of them after a prominent painter: Rembrandt, Vandyk, Rubens, Titian, and Raphaelle. Bearing those names and spurred on by their father, the boys, except for Vandyk who resisted the pressure, were bound to pursue a life of art. They, together with several other members of the numerous Peale clan, executed a great many still lifes. Raphaelle and Peale's younger brother, James, were both noted for their paintings of fruit.

Fruit, among other things, was depicted in the foreground of a famous nineteenth-century painting but it was the "other things" that were clearly the focus of attention. When Edouard Manet, one of the world's great masters, placed his canvas on exhibition he and his painting immediately became the eye of a stormy controversy that crackled through Paris. Consistent with its title—*Le Déjeuner sur l'Herbe* "Lunch on the Grass"—the canvas did indeed depict two couples picnicking in a wooded dell, a basket of fruit and other foods clearly presenting evidence of their gustatory intentions. What provoked the scandalized outbursts by both the press and the public was that the two men in the painting—easily recognizable as two well-known Parisians—were fully clothed while their two female companions were nude. It took many years before the arguments died away and the painting of the unorthodox picnic was accepted for what it really was, a masterpiece.

How food and art can become merged into one another was demonstrated vividly by an incident at an art exhibition in Berlin in 1908. Among the many works on display was a fine canvas by William Merritt Chase, an American artist hailed for his food paintings, many of which had been collected by museums. The Chase painting selected for showing in Berlin was of a fish, a subject that had for a long time fascinated the artist. The guest of honor at the exhibition was to be the Kaiser of Germany. When the monarch arrived the director proudly escorted him on a slow circuit of the gallery. Pausing in front of the Chase painting, the Kaiser said sourly, "This I do not like." Startled, the director replied, "But, your majesty, it is a fine painting by an eminent artist." Unimpressed, the Kaiser said, "I do not like fish. I do not eat fish." The crestfallen director was not imprudent enough to point out to the crowned head of Germany that he had been contemplating art, not his dinner.

But if poets, composers, sculptors, and painters have been carrying on a long-running love affair with food, so too have essayists, novelists, and dramatists. Harriet Beecher Stowe, author of *Uncle Tom's Cabin,* a blockbuster in its day, collaborated with her sister in writing a book devoted to food. Charles Lamb, the sparkling British essayist, wrote a delightfully lighthearted tribute to one of his favorite dishes, roast pork. The author of *The Three Musketeers, The Count of Monte Cristo,* and other major works, Alexandre Dumas, also wrote a monumental 1,000-page-plus volume devoted to a subject most dear to him: food.

And then there was William Shakespeare, idolized around the world as one of the most adroit and sensitive users of the English language. What has been less widely recognized is that he was also exceedingly deft in using food as a source of nourishment and enrichment for the language he employed. Threaded through all of his many works are food expressions that he wove into his text with skill and grace to convey special meanings in special ways. The world is my oyster, he has eaten me out of house and home, a dish fit for the gods, there's small choice in rotten apples, the ripest fruit falls first, the bitter bread of banishment, all of these—and scores more—are pure William Shakespeare.

Charles Dickens was another literary great who knew how to listen to food. To take the fat with the lean, and to be dead as mutton were two of the expressions he heard in the pantry of his mind. A third expression that he conceived and that has earned a permanent niche for itself in language has undergone a subtle change with the passage of time. Dickens is supposed to have said that one who is apologetic and self-effacing is eating humble pie. That isn't the way Dickens put it. What he actually said was that one who is meekly deferential is eating umble pie. The missing "h" is the key. In Dickens' time the innards of venison, known as "umbles," were never eaten by the master of the house or by members of his family; instead they were baked into a pie to feed to the servants. Because it was a dish considered fit only for the menials it is not difficult to see how Dickens' umble pie became the world's humble pie.

Curiously, at almost the exact moment that the rightful name of Dickens' pie was slipping from his grasp, a cake's name was at the center of a tug-of-war being waged by two rivals contending for its possession. The contest was being played out in Vienna, where food is never dismissed lightly. (The only prize that General Josef Radetzky considered worth taking back to Vienna from Italy where he commanded the Austrian army in the 1848 war was a breaded veal cutlet recipe—it became Austria's widely famed *Wiener schnitzel.*)

So when a noted hotel and an equally noted pastry shop contested each other over *Sachertorte,* a delectable chocolate cake that each claimed to have originated, the public divided itself into opposing factions. Finally the acrimonious debate was submitted to the courts for decision. The judicial authorities pondered long and ultimately conceived a solution that defused the situation. They declared both the hotel and the pastry shop to be winners in the case, granting each the right to use the *Sachertorte* name and recipe and to identify itself as the originator.

Disputes over food names have even invaded the august precincts of the United States Supreme Court. In 1893, a New York City importer who had been assessed customs duty on a shipment of tomatoes from the West Indies indignantly brought suit against the federal government to challenge the assessment. Building his case around the language of food, he based his suit on the contention that tomatoes are the fruit of the plant and that the Tariff Act of

1883 specifically exempted fruit from duty charges, unlike its treatment of vegetables which were not exempted.

The Justices listened solemnly while counsel for each side argued the merits of its position. Then they retired to their chambers to consider what a tomato really is. Ultimately the Justices arrived at a verdict that was worthy of a Solomon. They ruled that tomatoes are the fruit of the plant, botanically speaking, but are considered vegetables in the language of the kitchen and therefore, culinary usage taking precedence, are subject to customs assessment.

When the Justices of the Supreme Court ruled that one man's fruit is another's vegetable, they were simply giving legalistic credentials to an immutable culinary truth: what one sees on the pantry shelf depends entirely on how one looks at it. Smith, Rossini, Toulouse-Lautrec, Shakespeare, Dickens, and all the rest saw poetry, music, painting, sculpture, and literature. Others peering into the pantry have come away with different visions. They have glimpsed religion and mythology and magic, ingenuity and creativity, delicate refinement and vulgar excesses, coarseness and elegance, greed and passion, challenge and adventure, even humor. In a sense, humanity writes its autobiography at the dinner table.

One thing is certain beyond the possibility of argument. It is this: other interests may flag, other anxieties may resolve themselves, other loves may cool, but man's affair with his stomach is constant, pervasive, unabating, and ardent. It is well that God, in His infinite wisdom, granted only one stomach to each of us. Preoccupied as we are with that single stomach of ours, how would we ever be able to cope if He had given us two stomachs as He did the birds and the bees? Or, thinking the unthinkable, if He had granted each of us four as He did the cow?

INDEX

About the Author

VERNON PIZER is the author of numerous books and of several hundred articles in leading magazines in the United States, Europe, and the Far East. His work has been collected in anthologies, has been reprinted in many languages, and has been adopted as teaching aids by the U.S. Air Force Academy, Loyola University of Chicago, and many secondary schools.

The breadth of his interests is suggested by the variety of the subjects he has covered—foreign and military affairs, the sciences, social problems, sports, and travel—but the thread through all of his work is his emphasis on the people involved in the things he describes. His books include *Ink, Ark., and All That: How American Places Got Their Names; Glorious Triumphs: Athletes Who Conquered Adversity;* and *Take My Word for It,* a book about eponyms.

After having lived in Washington, Paris, Vienna, and Turkey, Mr. Pizer and his wife, Marguerite, now make their home in Georgia.